IMAGES
of America
SOQUEL

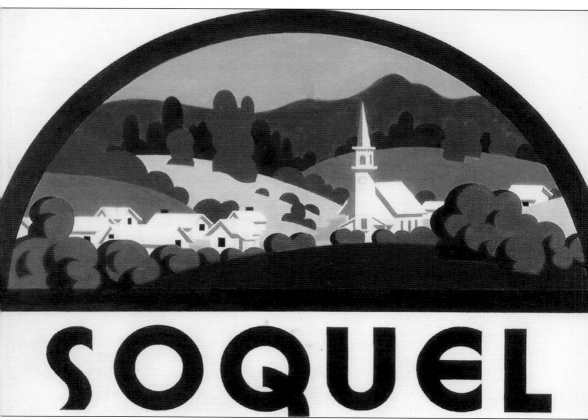

The sign was illustrated by artist Lee Blair (1911–1993). (Courtesy of Judy Parsons.)

ON THE COVER: Soquel Cash Store, offering general merchandise, was opened by Jarvis Esty and J. T. Lowry in the center of town about 1900. Esty became the sole owner in 1913. He was elected Santa Cruz County supervisor in 1896, dying in office in 1916. His son, Seward, was a partner in the business as a young man and for many years worked for the Associated Oil Company. Another son, Le Baron "Lee" Dill Esty (1875–1943), became a noted architect, designing the 1928 Independent Order of Odd Fellows (IOOF) building downtown as well as numerous structures throughout Santa Cruz County that are now listed on historic surveys. In the 1912 cover photograph, donated to the Soquel Pioneer and Historical Association by Jim Peters, are, from left to right, William Kropf, two unidentified, Billy Nash, Lee Esty, and Seward Esty. (Courtesy of the Soquel Pioneer and Historical Association.)

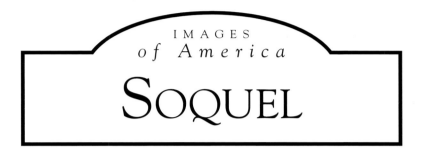

IMAGES
of America

SOQUEL

The Soquel Pioneer and Historical Association Book Committee
John Caldwell
Lynne McCall Caldwell
Alice Daubenbis
Barbara Harlamoff McCrary
Richard Nutter
Judy Parsons
Paul Parsons
Bill Roberson
Carolyn Swift
Judith Steen, Editor

ARCADIA
PUBLISHING

Published by Arcadia Publishing
Charleston, South Carolina

Printed in the United States of America

Library of Congress Control Number: 2009924705

For all general information, please contact Arcadia Publishing:
Telephone 843-853-2070
Fax 843-853-0044
E-mail sales@arcadiapublishing.com
For customer service and orders:
Toll-Free 1-888-313-2665

Visit us on the Internet at www.arcadiapublishing.com

This book is dedicated to Nora (Oliver) Angell (1867–1942), first president and founder of the Soquel Pioneer and Historical Association.

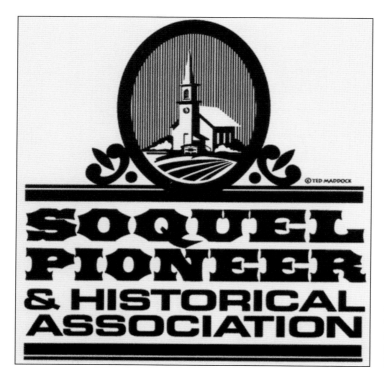

Artist Ted Maddock created this logo for the association. (Courtesy of the Soquel Pioneer and Historical Association.)

CONTENTS

ACKNOWLEDGMENTS

The authors are grateful to all those who have supplied photographs, research, and expertise in the four-year endeavor to create this publication. They are further thankful for the skillful guidance of our editor, Judith Steen; supportive help from Amy Dunning of the Museum of Art and History and from Sandy Lydon, historian emeritus, Cabrillo College; ongoing assistance from the Capitola Historical Museum; and proficient scanning provided by Image Management Services. Unless otherwise noted, all images appear courtesy of the Soquel Pioneer and Historical Association. Other photograph contributors are acknowledged in the courtesy lines that follow each caption.

INTRODUCTION

Soquel residents are accustomed to coaching visitors in the correct pronunciation of the name of their town. It is "so-kel" but never, ever "so-kwel."

The names of only three existing communities in Santa Cruz County can be traced to the local Indians: Soquel, Zayante, and Aptos. Pronunciations are tricky for each of them.

Historically, Soquel identifies a people and their place, although the exact origin of the word remains unclear. It is believed to be a Spanish corruption of the name of the Uypi Indian leader Suquer, the second person to be baptized at the Santa Cruz Mission, established in 1791. Among the attempts to record into Spanish and English what was thought to be the original Uypi name are such articulations as Sauquil, Shoquel, Osocales, and Usacalis.

The Uypi were an Ohlone tribelet. The tribelet boundaries extended to the banks of the river now known as Soquel Creek. The building of a mission 4 miles away foreshadowed the loss of Uypi customs and their way of life. Now, more than 200 years later, lingering cultural threads are being rewoven to continue their story.

Once within the mission compound, Native American converts, called neophytes, died rapidly from disease and poor nutrition. By the time the missions were ordered secularized in 1833, only a few of the original native inhabitants remained in the region. None from within the present boundaries of Soquel were known to be among them.

In 1797, the establishment of a neighboring settlement, Villa de Branciforte, deepened the impact. Built within a mile of the mission, the town was a soldier-settler outpost founded with the dual purpose of colonization and defense. Some of the first arrivals had been convicted of petty crimes, while most were soldiers who had finished their term of enlistment with the Spanish government and were now settlers arriving with families.

Few references to Soquel appeared in early documents. One mention, in 1803, referred to a Branciforte resident, Marcelino Bravo, and his request for permission to graze cattle while living at "el rio de Bravo o Shoquel." He died before an answer was given.

No other residents are recorded within the boundaries of present-day Soquel until after 1822, when government control of Alta California shifted from Spain to Mexico and new land-use patterns emerged. When the Mexican government began issuing rancho land grants after mission secularization, Villa de Branciforte's retired military and their offspring were the chief recipients.

Foreigners, or *extranjeros*, began to appear more often during this era. A number of them, particularly sailors, married women from the villa and adopted the lifestyle of the original colonists and their descendants.

Others who came in the late 1840s, often viewed as loutish and greedy, were frontiersmen who traveled overland and favored conquest over assimilation. Setting themselves in conflict with the Spanish-speaking inhabitants of the region, the newcomers assisted in the American takeover of 1846. Following statehood in 1850, they were joined by hundreds of others who wanted to build English-speaking communities patterned after New England settlements.

Established in 1852, Soquel was typical of towns in the West that were created soon after the Gold Rush. The village mushroomed in size as miners left the goldfields and tapped the region's natural resources. By 1860, Soquel was the third largest settlement in Santa Cruz County, challenging both Santa Cruz and Watsonville for greater prominence.

Soquel Creek shaped both the town and its economy. The stream provided waterpower for manufacturing and supplied at least five sawmills several miles upstream from town. Where the creek met the ocean, the beach flat known as Soquel Landing became an important shipping point. A wharf built in 1857 was soon linked to Soquel by roads that continued beyond, either to Watsonville or Santa Cruz or up through the mountains on the Soquel Turnpike to San Jose.

By 1868, Pacific Coast Steamship Company freighters were docking regularly at the landing to take aboard immense loads of lumber, leather, manufactured goods, and produce.

As first-growth redwoods were cut and stumps cleared, Soquel Valley lands were planted in crops. Farmers experimented with potatoes, wheat, sugar beets, corn, and barley. Apple and cherry orchards and vineyards took root.

One of the most successful local enterprises was built at the beach, where shipbuilder Samuel Alonzo Hall set up a small tent campground on land he leased from Soquel Landing's owner, Frederick Augustus Hihn. Hall's Camp Capitola officially opened in 1874, the same summer a railroad trestle was built over Soquel Creek near the beach. The founding of the resort and the overlapping construction of the Santa Cruz–Watsonville Railroad dramatically impacted Soquel. Without close proximity to the rail line and unable to share in the greater fortunes of a tourist economy, the town's expansion slowed down.

Although separate, Soquel and Capitola remained allied. Outside the seasonal beach resort, the two were joined in an unbroken landscape of small farms, bulb and flower fields, chicken ranches, and orchards of cherries and apples.

Permanent and visible dividers appeared in 1949, when Capitola incorporated as a municipality just a few months before Highway 1 was completed. The high-speed thoroughfare set down a wide swath of pavement, cutting through roads and splitting neighborhoods.

Nevertheless, the character of Soquel extends even now toward the sea, and a shared connection with Capitola remains.

One

GRASS ROOTS
LAND, LIFESTYLE, AND LANGUAGE

Before the arrival of the Spanish, the native people of the Central California Coast lived in culturally diverse tribal units of 100 to 250 members. Known today as the Ohlone, they shared the landscape with seals, sea lions, deer, elk, grizzly bears, coyotes, and a variety of other animals. They ate meat and fish, roots and berries, and acorns, an important staple. The inhabitants lived in villages that grew, dwindled, or were abandoned at different seasons as families shifted locations to fish, harvest plants, and hunt animals. They burned coastal lands to assist the growth of seed-bearing plants and to enrich grazing sites for deer and other game.

Living in the territory of present-day Santa Cruz and Soquel, the Uypi, like other Ohlone tribal groups, spoke differing dialects of a common language. They viewed themselves as an independent territorial unit, although they intermarried, communicated, and traded with their neighbors.

Between 1770 and 1797, the Spanish came with the Franciscan friars, who established six missions in Alta California. Forced to learn Spanish and to act as citizens of Spain, the Native Americans were treated as dependents of the mission. Native American children were routinely abducted and baptized, and the parents who came after them were also drawn into the mission system. In time, all freedom was lost. With secularization, most of the land now in Santa Cruz County was transferred to the Californios. Many of the native survivors were pressed into labor on the ranchos.

English-speaking arrivals in the 1840s introduced conflicting values, prejudices, and laws. The newcomers rapaciously took up the small parcels belonging to the Native Americans. Separated from their lands, traditions, and language, the Ohlone population continued to withdraw and diminish. Reclaiming the past is today the ongoing work of their descendants and regional historians.

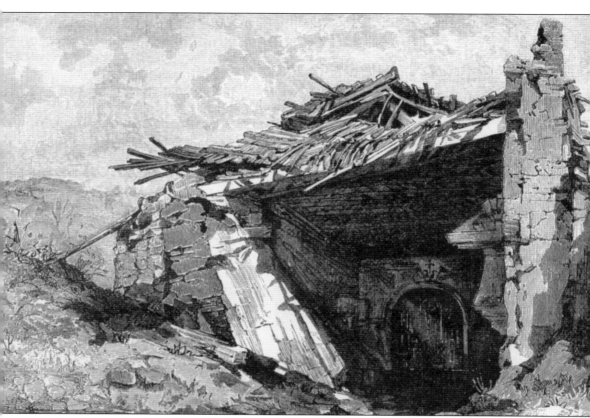

Twelfth in the chain along the El Camino Real, Santa Cruz Mission was founded in 1791 by Fr. Fermin Francisco de Lasuen, successor to Fr. Junipero Serra as head of the Missions of Alta California. The mission reached its peak in 1796, when the population rose to 523 neophytes. Numbers declined rapidly thereafter. Ownership of mission lands shifted when Gov. Jose Figueroa secularized the Santa Cruz Mission in 1834. After the American takeover in 1846 and statehood in 1850, English-speaking pioneers introduced their preference for New England–style architecture. The mission chapel was already crumbling when it collapsed in 1857. This illustration by Mary Hallock Foote is from a watercolor drawing by Mrs. Matthias published in "A Sea-Port on the Pacific," *Scribner's Monthly*, August 1878. (Courtesy of the Capitola Historical Museum.)

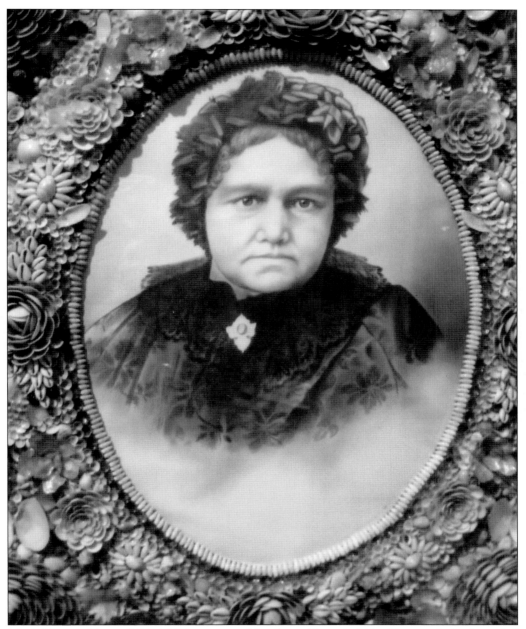

Maria Martina Castro (1807–1890) was a granddaughter of Joaquin Isidro Castro, who had traveled with his family to Alta California with the Anza party in 1776. Baptized at Villa de Branciforte, Martina grew up there and, in 1824, wed soldier Simon Cota. She became a widow with two children within six years. In 1831, she married Irish sailor Michael Lodge. The couple was granted title in 1833 to the 1,668-acre Rancho Soquel (Shoquel), a 2-mile strip along the coast. A decade later, approval of the Rancho Soquel (Shoquel) Augmentation allowed an expansion of up to 32,702 acres in the forested mountains. Although Michael knew the potential of redwood timber, the Lodges primarily valued their flat land for grazing cattle. Hides were shipped regularly from the beach, known then as La Playa de Soquel. (Courtesy of the Museum of Art and History.)

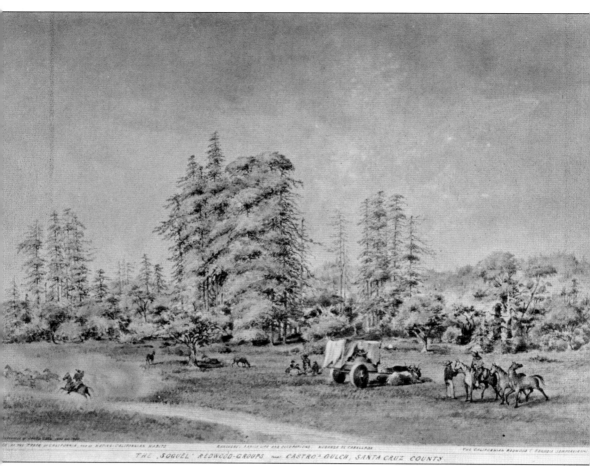

A lithograph by Edward Vischer titled *Castro's Gulch* depicts Soquel redwoods, vaqueros (cowboys), and a *carreta*, a heavy wooden cart with rough-hewn seats and a rawhide top. The carreta transported families and products such as "California banknotes" (cattle hides) used for trade with ships from foreign ports. Vischer's early illustration portrays the rancho lands of Martina Castro Lodge and her brother Rafael Castro, who owned neighboring Rancho Aptos to the east. A conflict over grazing land prompted Lodge to apply for the augmentation. After California statehood and the distribution of Martina's property to her children in 1850, the augmentation's boundaries and deeds were contested in court over a period of years. (Courtesy of the California Historical Society.)

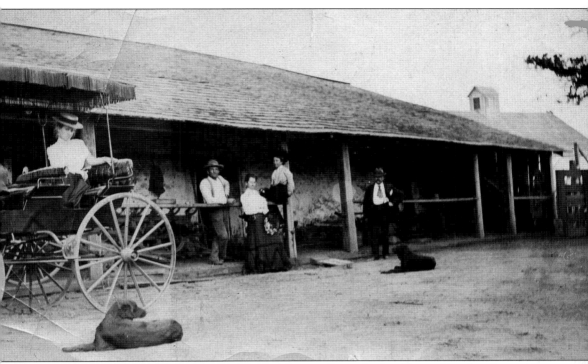

The Gold Rush triggered devastating events for Martina Castro Lodge. She and her family joined the migration to mining country, where they established a general store. When the three youngest Lodge children died of fever, Martina returned home. Her husband followed, but he vanished and was presumed murdered. Unable to read, write, or speak English, the rancho grantee faced the grueling process of proving title to her ranchos in the American court. Seeking protection, Martina married once again, to Louis Depeaux. She was betrayed by Depeaux, several family members, church and elected officials, attorneys, and land-hungry settlers. She was deprived of her land, her personal belongings, her cultural way of life, and for a time, her freedom. The 1903 photograph of the Castro-Lodge adobe shows the Augustus Noble family, who acquired the property in 1856. The adobe, demolished in 1925, was located on Hill Street in present-day Capitola.

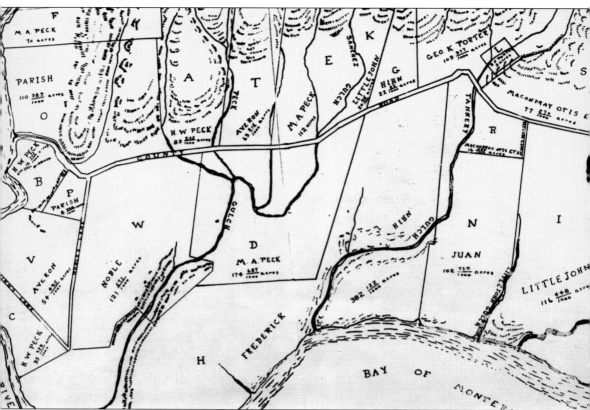

Once California became a state, Martina Castro Lodge divided her lands into equal parts for herself and eight surviving children. Each received one-ninth of Rancho Soquel and one-ninth of the Rancho Soquel Augmentation. Most of the family soon sold their shares for the cash needed to adapt to the American economy. Five of Martina's daughters, for example, sold their augmentation territories to capitalist Frederick Hihn. Another, Carmel Lodge Fallon, sold her Rancho Soquel holdings to pioneer Joshua Parrish, while her augmentation property—located today in the Forest of Nisene Marks—went to a lumber company. An 1868 Santa Cruz County map shows the boundaries of Castro family heirs (Peck, Littlejohn, Juan, and Averon) alongside those of Soquel settlers. Noble Lane is today Capitola Avenue, while Hihn's Lane is Bay Avenue. The county road is Soquel Drive.

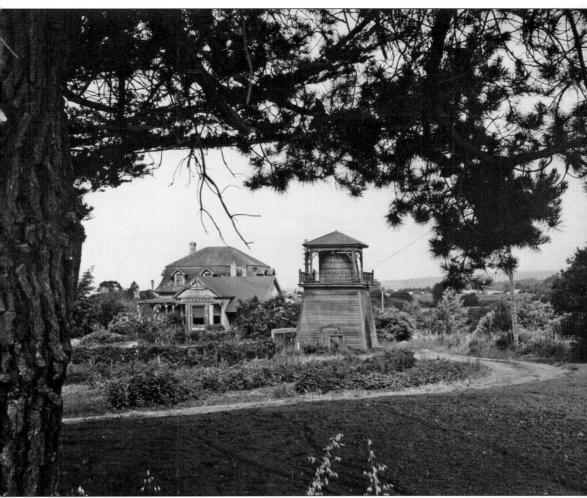

Maria Guadalupe Lodge, the youngest daughter, married Joseph Averon. They were childless but raised the daughters of Maria's brother, Michael Lodge II. The couple, along with family members living close by, took care of Martina in her last years. She was able to live by herself in an orchard cottage near the Averon home, where she died in December 1890. Most of the Averon property was partitioned and sold over time. A viticulturist from France, Joseph Averon kept a vineyard and winery near their house, which stands today along Capitola Avenue, behind the Capitola Mansion Apartments. The small, Victorian front addition included in this 1950s photograph has been demolished. The mansard-roofed section at the rear is the oldest residence within Capitola city boundaries. (Courtesy of Tom King.)

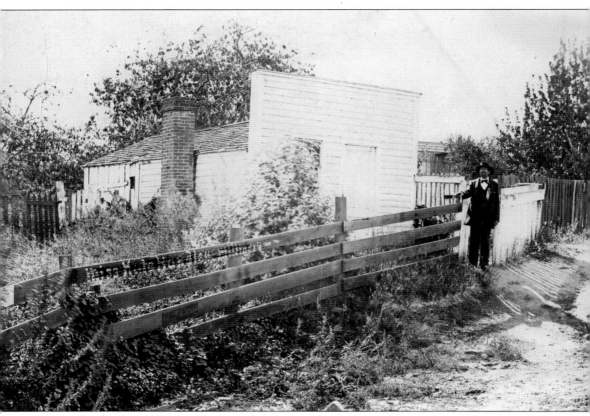

John Daubenbiss (1816–1896), above, left Bavaria for the United States in 1835. Landing in New York, the 19-year-old eventually came west to California, arriving in 1843. Daubenbiss settled in San Jose and became a naturalized Mexican citizen. Together with John Hames (1813–1883), he built a mill for Mariano Vallejo near the Mission San Jose in 1845. The next year, Daubenbiss and Hames made an agreement with Rancho Soquel owners Michael and Martina Castro Lodge to construct a sawmill on the east bank of the Soquel River. The mill—although destroyed by a flood within the year—signaled the beginning of the economic shift from cattle raising to forest-based industry that would take place within the next decade.

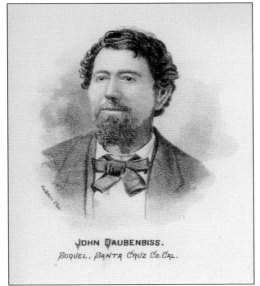

JOHN DAUBENBISS.
Soquel, Santa Cruz Co. Cal.

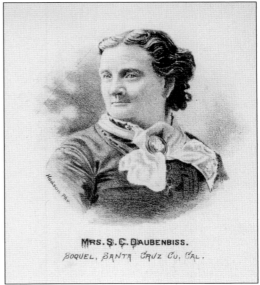

MRS. S. C. DAUBENBISS.
Soquel, Santa Cruz Cu. Cal.

In 1845, Daubenbiss and Hames acquired from Alexander Rodriguez most of the 1,473-acre Rancho Arroyo del Rodeo between the west bank of Soquel Creek and Rodeo Gulch. Daubenbiss joined Fremont's Battalion during the war between the United States and Mexico. After returning to Soquel in 1847, he married Sarah C. Lard of Santa Clara, built two gristmills, donated a cemetery and a school, and served several terms as county supervisor. The above is a lithograph from W. W. Elliott's *Santa Cruz County, California, Illustrations, with Historical Sketch*, 1879. (Courtesy of the Capitola Historical Museum.)

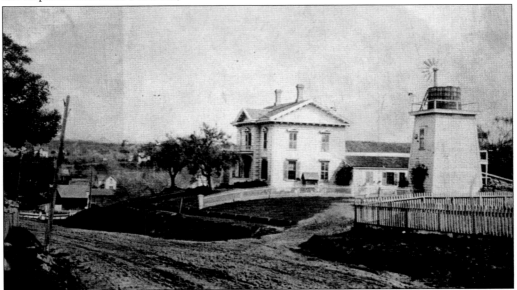

John Daubenbiss built a small house on his 1,100-acre farm above Soquel Creek in 1847–1848. Twenty years later, architect Thomas Beck designed a two-story, Italianate-style front addition. Daubenbiss, who had experienced the destructive force of floodwater, wisely chose a home site up the hillside on the west bank. The structure was renovated in 1977, and along with the Soquel Congregational Church, it remains a prominent town landmark.

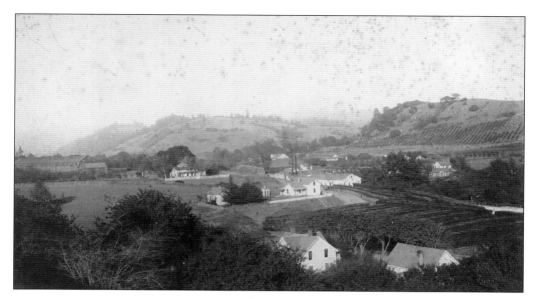

In 1847, John Hames, 35, married Drusilla Shadden, 14. He was appointed alcalde (mayor) before joining the Gold Rush and served as county supervisor in 1852 and 1859–1860. The family settled along Porter Street on the west side of the creek. Although much of his property was forfeited later, Hames remained active in the Soquel community until shortly before his death. The undated photograph above was taken from Hames Hill showing the home site and the flour mill buildings that later became the South Coast Paper Mill. In the late-1880s view below, taken from the hill looking south toward the village, Soquel's busiest intersection has a tree in the center of the county road. This incongruity obviously changed as traffic increased. Ned Porter's warehouse, jutting into the roadway at center, created a building footprint that remains to this day.

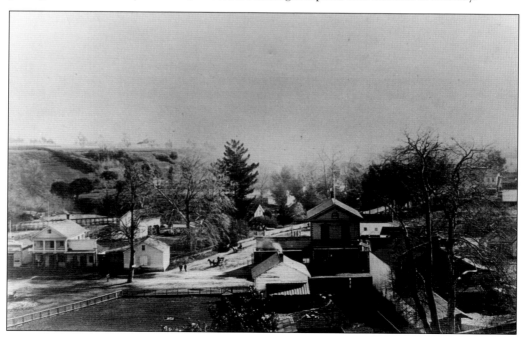

Two

INDUSTRY
RED GOLD, RAWHIDES,
AND WRAPPING PAPER

Gold discovery in 1848 brought thousands of fortune-seekers to California, but not all succeeded. Another form of wealth was discovered in "red gold," the massive redwood tree, *Sequoia sempervirens*, which grew prolifically along the coastal corridors. Sawmills sprang up rapidly in the Santa Cruz Mountains along their stream courses. Timber harvesting was Soquel's core industry, leading to the hum and whir of other trades.

Logging was so extensive in the mountains that the town, founded in 1852, emerged by 1860 as the county's third largest settlement. Occupations kept pace with a labor force that attracted a community of young families. Flour mills, tanneries, chair factories, a shoe manufacturing plant, a wool-pulling mill, a beet sugar plant, and a paper mill were among the early industries that nourished the pocketbooks of local workers.

La Playa de Soquel became Soquel Landing. For many years, the wharf was piled high with shipments of lumber and redwood products—shingles, shakes, fence posts, split pickets, wharf piles, and telephone poles. Across the bridges that skirted downtown Soquel, wagonloads were channeled for shipment by sea on coastal freighters like the 239-foot *Gypsy* (*Gipsy*).

Nearby, small fishing colonies were established along the coastline. A great field of kelp floated near the shore, and beyond it a famed fishing ground yielded a variety of fish in vast numbers. Whales were often seen and sometimes hunted. Fishermen had to depend on local markets until construction of a rail line allowed shipments of thousands of pounds of fish per year to far-away destinations.

The railroad's construction promised further expansion. When it arrived in 1876, however, the route ran along the coastline and crossed, wherever possible, the lands of farsighted capitalist Frederick Hihn. The Soquel depot was built near the wharf and the promising new resort of Camp Capitola. Later, when the line was purchased by Southern Pacific Railroad in 1881, the station was shifted to the eastern end of the trestle. The name was by then forever linked to Capitola.

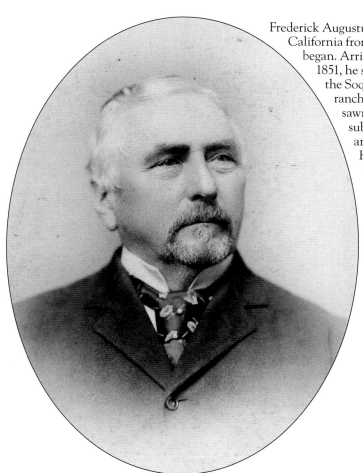

Frederick Augustus Hihn (1829–1913) sailed to California from Germany as the Gold Rush began. Arriving in Santa Cruz County in 1851, he soon acquired vast sections of the Soquel and Soquel Augmentation ranchos. As the shrewd developer of sawmills, water works, turnpikes, subdivisions, railroads, banks, and numerous other businesses, Hihn was a major influence on the future Santa Cruz County, including Soquel and Camp Capitola. (Courtesy of the Capitola Historical Museum.)

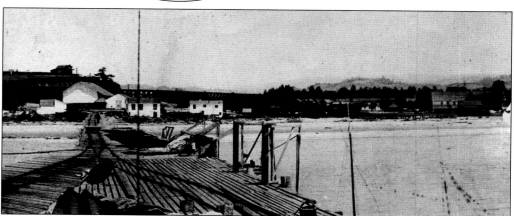

When Hihn bought Rancho Arroyo del Rodeo land on the west side of Soquel Creek in 1857, he had a 450-foot wharf built to ship lumber to market. Pacific Coast Steamship Company freighters made regular landings, and imported goods were hauled to a warehouse at the end of Wharf Road. Once the Santa Cruz–Watsonville Railroad was completed in 1876, shipments by sea gradually diminished. (Courtesy of the Capitola Historical Museum.)

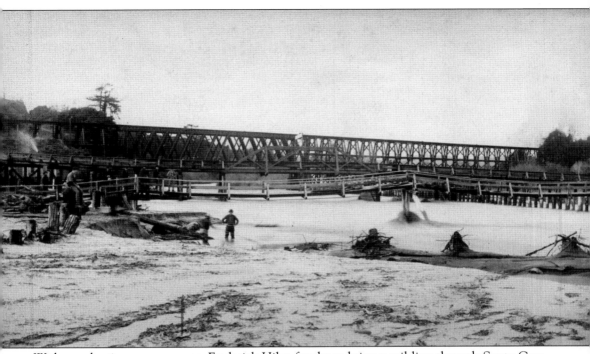

With unrelenting perseverance, Frederick Hihn fought to bring a rail line through Santa Cruz County. His goal was to connect it to a statewide rail network. Once he succeeded, a 900-foot trestle hovered over the agricultural fields at the coast, a mile from Soquel. Although the depot location proved to be an unfortunate one for Soquel, the railroad was still a boon to local industry. The wintertime scene above, about 1890, illustrates the seasonal power of Soquel Creek. The pedestrian cable footbridge and wagon bridge were built to serve Camp Capitola, which—for good reason—remained closed in the off-season. In the months between September and May, the shoreline was still considered by Soquelites to be a part of their town. (Courtesy of Alice Daubenbis.)

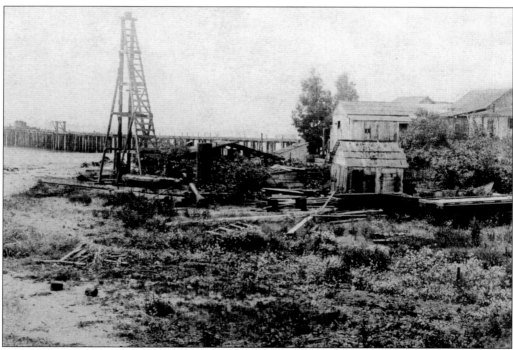

Capt. John Davenport (1818–1892) sailed to California in 1851 and established the state's first shore whaling company in Monterey. Moving to Soquel Landing in 1865, he set up rendering pots on the beach with little success. Relocating up the coast the next year, he ultimately founded Davenport's Landing in a small cove north of the present-day town that bears his name. (Courtesy of Richard Dietz and the Davenport/North Coast Reunion Committee.)

Shipments by sea from Soquel Landing slowed over time, and wharf pilings were often lost in storms. Even so, the fishermen leasing land from F. A. Hihn eked out a living, settling with their families in a cluster of shacks at the end of the pier. From 1890 to 1920, most were Italian immigrants from Riva Trigoso, a remote community on the Ligurian coast. (Courtesy of Gordon Van Zuiden.)

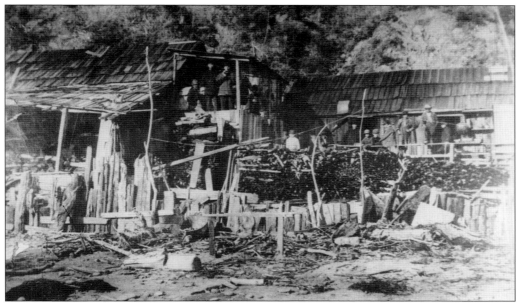

Chinese fishermen began working along the Santa Cruz County coastline in the 1850s. The men leased a site from F. A. Hihn along the bluffs east of Capitola. They fished with seine and gill nets and trawling lines, shipping their catch to market by train after 1876. This c. 1889 photograph is the only known image of the China Beach settlement, which survived through the early 1890s. (Courtesy of the Capitola Historical Museum.)

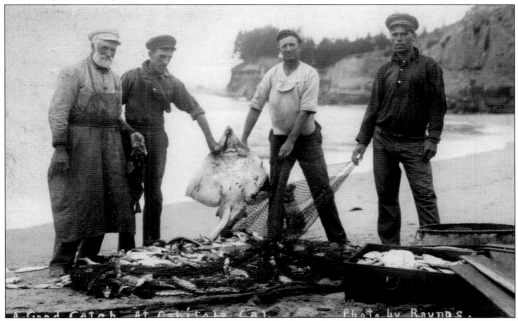

Capt. Thomas Lindsay of Ireland, far left, arrived in America in 1879 after a life at sea. He and his wife, Arabella, raised their family near the wharf, where Lindsay was in charge of operations and repair. In 1894, he established the Soquel Seining Company, leasing China Beach from Hihn. Today the site is part of New Brighton Beach State Park. (Courtesy of Gordon Van Zuiden.)

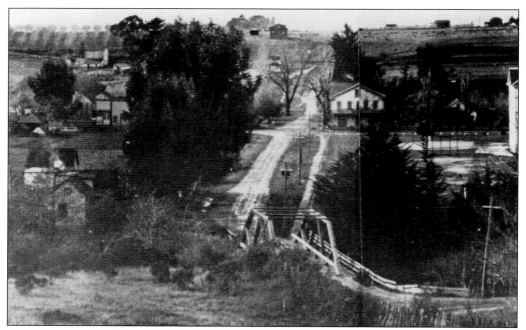

Soquel's earliest sawmill was at a curve in the creek near the Walnut Street Bridge, shown in this mid-1890s photograph. Built by John Daubenbiss and John Hames, the mill was briefly operated by Henry Hill and Guadalupe Castro, a brother of Martina Castro Lodge, until it washed away in 1847. Adna A. Hecox (1806–1883), a carpenter and minister, was hired by Michael Lodge to construct a replacement, upstream to the north.

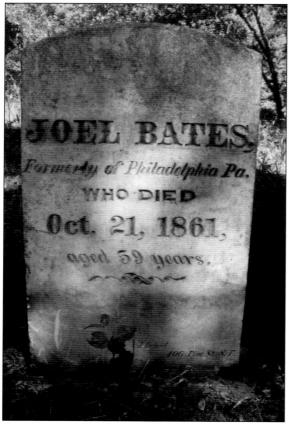

JOEL BATES,
Formerly of Philadelphia Pa.
WHO DIED
Oct. 21, 1861,
aged 59 years.

Born in New Jersey, Joel Bates (1801–1861) settled in Soquel about 1853. Five years later, he built a steam-powered sawmill along a tributary of Soquel Creek named for him. Although Bates died, the mill continued operating until 1866. Bates Creek water was used by Frederick Hihn, who supplied it in the 1880s to both Soquel and Camp Capitola. Bates's headstone is one of the oldest in the Soquel Cemetery.

In 1861, the Grover brothers—James Lyman (right), Stephen Freeland (Frealon), and Whitney—along with James Lyman's son, Dwight W., bought 800 acres along Bates Creek. Two miles north of Soquel Village, in 1866, they built a sawmill. The site soon became known as Grover's Gulch. Over time, they owned two more Soquel mills, with others at Porter Gulch, Scotts Valley, Brookdale, Majors Creek, Little Basin, and Gazos Creek in San Mateo County.

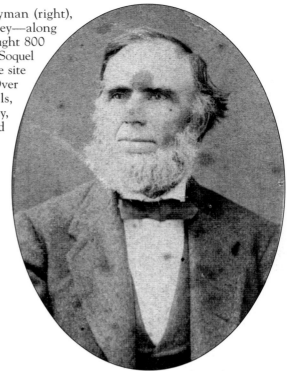

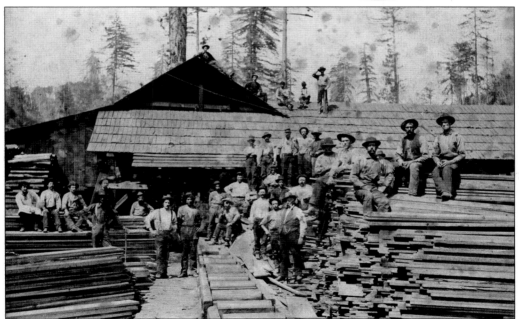

Phyllis Bertorelli Patten grew up in Grover's Gulch. In her history, entitled *Oh That Reminds Me . . .*, she noted that Grover's Mill typically employed 50 to 60 men, some as young as 15. The pay was $1.50 for a 12-hour day, with 50¢ deducted for those who took room and board. Today Grover's Gulch is the Glen Haven community. In the photograph, Stephen Grover is in front, wearing a vest.

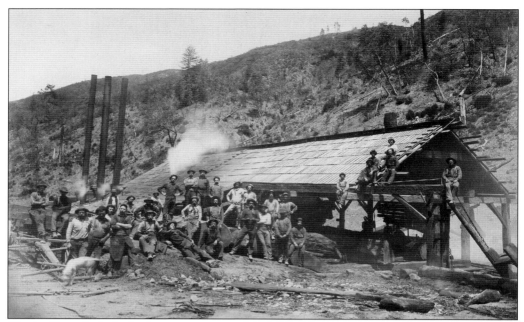

Charles Henry Ryder built a large steam-powered sawmill in the mountains at the head of Soquel Creek. The background of this *c.* 1897 image shows how heavily early-day loggers cut the timber. William R. "Billy" Jones, the mill's blacksmith, came from Kansas about 1890. He is in the front row with his arms across his chest, slightly to the right of the dog. (Courtesy of the William R. Jones family.)

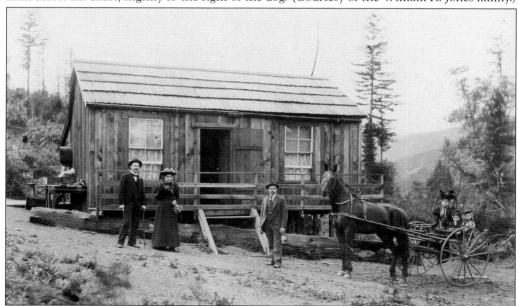

Sunday at Ryder's mill often meant receiving visitors, in this case Frank Cook and family. William R. Jones, left, stands with a handmade cane in this 1897 photograph. The small redwood cabin, board-and-batten with a barn-shake roof, was typical of a woodsman's residence at a mill or a "split-stuff" camp. Occasionally remnants of one can still be found, more than 110 years later. (Courtesy of the William R. Jones family.)

George K. Porter (1833–1906) of Duxbury, Massachusetts, arrived in Soquel with his cousin Edward "Ned" Porter in 1853. George purchased a tannery east of Soquel and went into partnership with another cousin, Ben Porter. From 1860 to 1863, George served as state senator from Santa Cruz and Monterey Counties. His home remains as a landmark on Soquel Drive near Porter Gulch Road and Cabrillo College. (Courtesy of the Benjamin Porter family.)

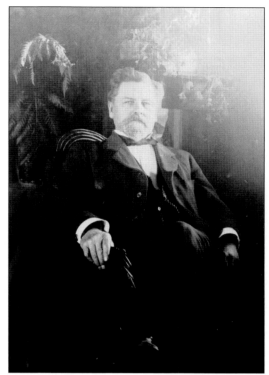

Vermont native Benjamin Franklin Porter (1834–1905) arrived in Soquel in 1853. He worked in a sawmill until he became a partner in his cousin George Porter's tannery. Historian Hubert Bancroft, who interviewed Benjamin at age 90, said that as a successful businessman, he had "no more ostentation or pretensions as the banker and manufacturer than he had as Ben the wood chopper and shingle maker." (Courtesy of the Benjamin Porter family.)

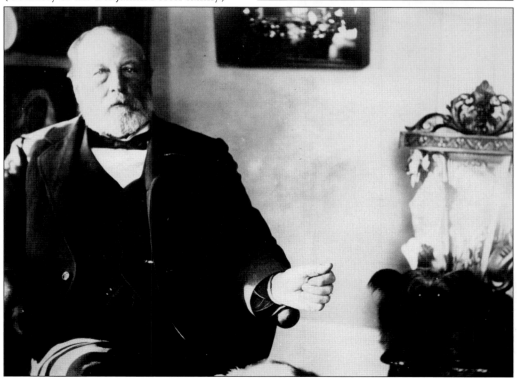

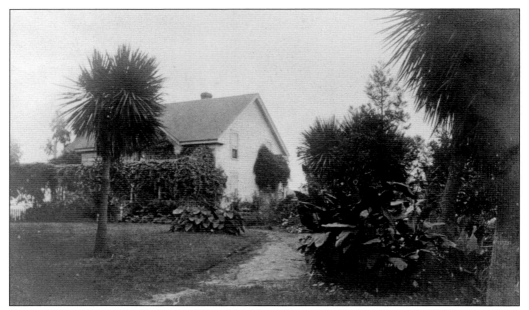

Benjamin and his wife, Catherine "Kate" Hubbard Porter, built their home in 1872 across from the tannery. The site today is part of Cabrillo College. Porter eventually held multiple interests in business and farming. The only time he was known to carry a weapon was when he went to polling places during the Civil War and was expecting a raid on the ballot boxes. (Courtesy of the Benjamin Porter family.)

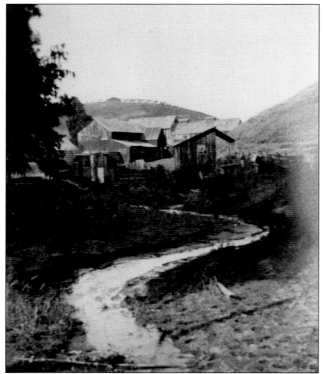

Benjamin Porter's brother Ned (1826–1908) was a founder of the Soquel business district. George Porter's brother John became county sheriff in 1857 and later helped shape the commercial and agricultural life of the Pajaro Valley. Another brother, Frank, was the Porter Tannery superintendent in the 1860s. The site of the tannery and sawmill at Porter Gulch is shown in this photograph, taken about 1900. (Courtesy of the Benjamin Porter family.)

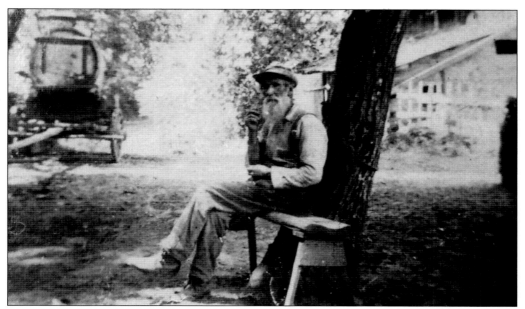

George E. Olive, a forty-niner from New Brunswick, Canada, operated a sawmill in the 1890s near today's Olive Springs on Hinckley Creek. It was located near the Hinckley–Soquel Creek confluence, several miles north of town. Some time before 1897, he developed the site as a campground. Cold water with sulphur, soda, iron, and magnesium was advertised for its medicinal values. (Courtesy of Ron Olmstead and the Van Dorsten family.)

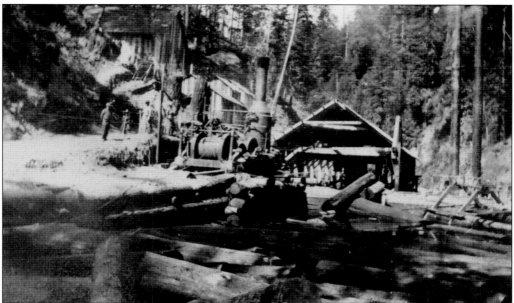

Moving logs at the Olive Springs mill was done with a "steam donkey." Its stack and winch drum are shown in this 1898 photograph. Logs were dragged out of the forest, and the "donkeys" moved by winching themselves from place to place. They were the industrial replacement for ox teams and were used extensively in late 19th- and early 20th-century logging operations. (Courtesy of Ron Olmstead.)

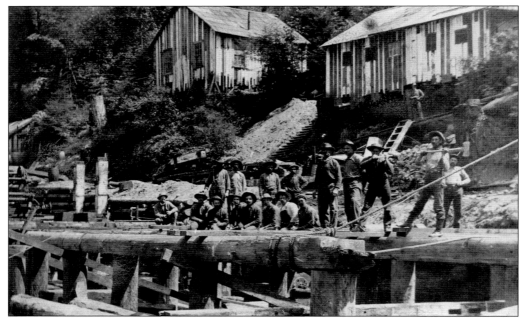

Loma Prieta Lumber Company's sawmill on Hinckley Creek was destroyed by flooding during the winter of 1905–1906. Reconstruction was progressing when this photograph was taken just before the April 1906 earthquake, a tragic event that inundated the mill with mud, burying alive nine men and a dog.

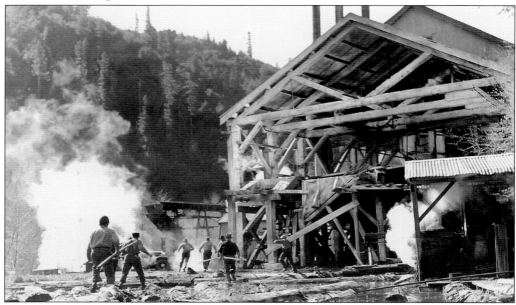

Monterey Bay Redwood Company was located at the end of Olive Springs Road in the 1930s. The company used modern equipment to produce 50,000–70,000 board feet per day and employed 50–100 workers. The mill was a location for the film *The Forest Rangers* (1942) with Fred MacMurray, Susan Hayward, and Paulette Goddard. This photograph was taken during an action scene. (Courtesy of Big Creek Lumber Company, Lud McCrary collection.)

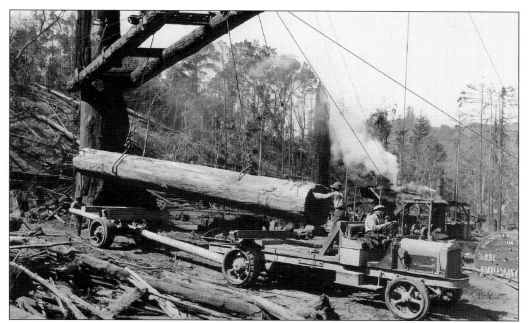

Monterey Bay Redwood Company was one of the first local lumber companies to use truck logging. Logs were loaded on a truck with a boom rigged on a spar tree. A cable powered by a steam donkey, visible in the background, accomplished the lifting. The operation closed when the timber gave out shortly after the end of World War II. (Courtesy of Big Creek Lumber Company, Lud McCrary collection.)

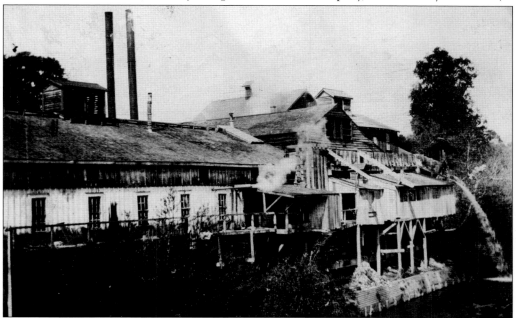

Originally the site of a flour mill built by John Hames and John Daubenbiss, South Coast Paper Mill on Paper Mill Road was established in 1879–1880 by Edward and Frank O'Neill (O'Neil). Newspaper columnist Ernest Otto, writing in 1941, recalled when the region was "one field of grain after another" and said that local straw was used at the mill to create a brown "butcher's paper."

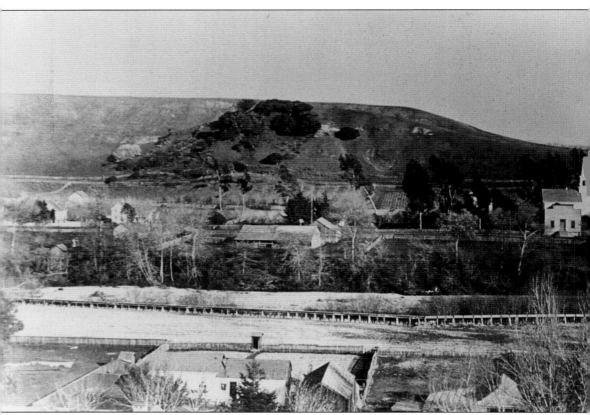

Frederick Hihn negotiated with the O'Neill brothers in the mid-1880s to run a flume down Soquel Creek toward the beach. Liquid chemicals from the paper mill and sewage from Soquel School streamed down the chute to a point above Capitola (near today's Riverview Avenue). Outhouses for the tent campground were built over it. The sludge was then directed underground and eastward through a 300-foot tunnel drilled under Depot Hill. In this way, effluent was discharged toward Aptos and into the bay, about 200 feet east of the campground. The flume allowed Hihn's resort at Capitola to enjoy a reasonably clean water environment. The photograph shows the paper mill flume at the center.

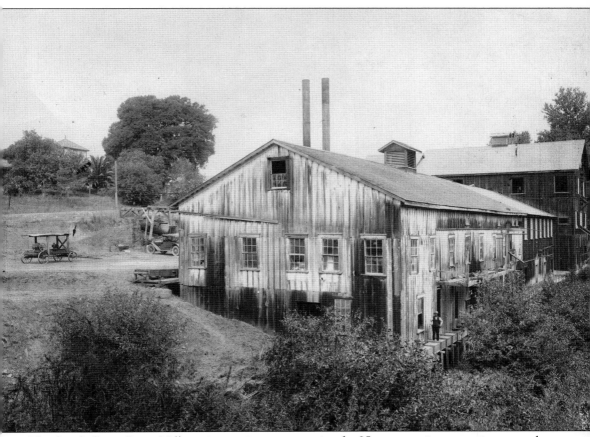

The South Coast Paper Mill was in continuous operation for 25 years, at times running around the clock, producing 800 tons of paper annually, using 1,800 tons of straw, 2,000 cords of wood, and 1,900 barrels of lime. In later years, as grain fields were converted to orchards, rags and used paper were shipped to Capitola by steamer for use at the mill. After 1904, it functioned sporadically. During World War I, C. W. Callaghan, one of the mill's owners, shipped most of the paper output to China to be used for firecrackers. An attempt was later made at the mill to convert rice hulls into paper. The plant was last used between 1927 and 1931 in an experiment to make pulp berry boxes. An estimated 200,000 feet of "first class lumber" were salvaged after the mill's demolition in 1934.

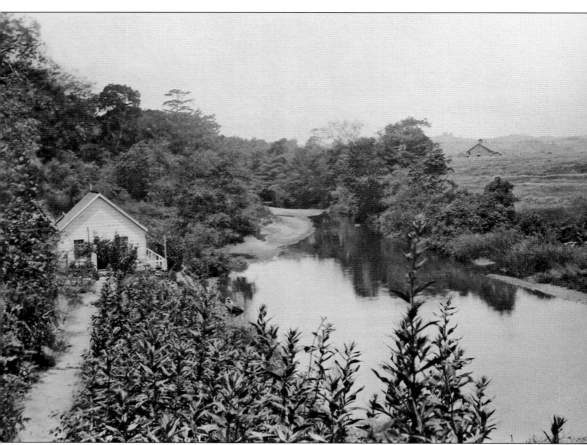

The California Beet Sugar Company relocated its factory from Alvarado to Soquel in 1874. Supt. Andreas Otto arrived with the machinery from Germany. Landowner Frederick Hihn provided a portion of the crop and the wood to fuel the mill, while John T. Porter supplied beets from 400 acres planted on his ranch in Pajaro. The three-and-a-half-story mill was located on a 30-acre tract between Riverview and Bay Avenues in present-day Capitola. Chinese workers were the majority of the 200-man crew employed in the factory and the fields. The photograph, taken about 1887, shows a glimpse of the mill's barn in the distance at right. (Courtesy of the Polhemus family, Edith C. Smith Collection, Sourisseau Academy, San Jose State University.)

Three

AGRICULTURE
THE GOOD EARTH

Because their lands were isolated along the California coastline, Soquel settlers knew they needed to be self-sufficient and raise a major portion of their food supply.

A Mediterranean climate—which allowed for a long growing season—meant that most of their needs were met though efficient land use. Families raised chickens for meat and eggs, cows for milk and cheese, and vegetables, including root crops, which could be stored over winter. Surplus goods were traded or sold to neighbors and local markets. Produce was also shipped to San Francisco from Soquel Landing, today's wharf at Capitola.

The terrain, with the exception of the coastal plains near the bay, was not well suited to large-scale agricultural plantings. These areas were used to grow cereal crops and sugar beets. Once the hilly areas were logged for timber, they were cleared of stumps and the land was planted in orchards, vineyards, and field crops.

Apples were the primary tree fruit planted because of their versatility, long shelf life, and shipping ability. They could be used fresh, dried, or for juice such as cider and vinegar. Apple dryers were major employers of local labor.

Soquel became known for production of cherries, pears, plums, and prunes. As transportation improved, local crops were trucked to markets in San Francisco and Los Angeles. Cherries, which are labor intensive and require a large farm labor source, were picked by workers, including immigrants from China, Mexico, and during the 1930s, the Midwest, when refugees arrived from the Dust Bowl to seek work in local fields.

Farmers continually sought new ways to increase their income. In the 1920s, plums, strawberries, and bulbs were profitable choices. Gladiolus grown for both flowers and bulbs were raised by many Soquel farmers. Violets were hybridized along the banks of Soquel Creek.

Agriculture remained the primary economic engine until the end of World War II, when a trend began to subdivide farmland for housing. Ornamental plants for nurseries were grown on acreage once used for sizeable orchards. By the 1950s, surrounding tracts were being developed for homes.

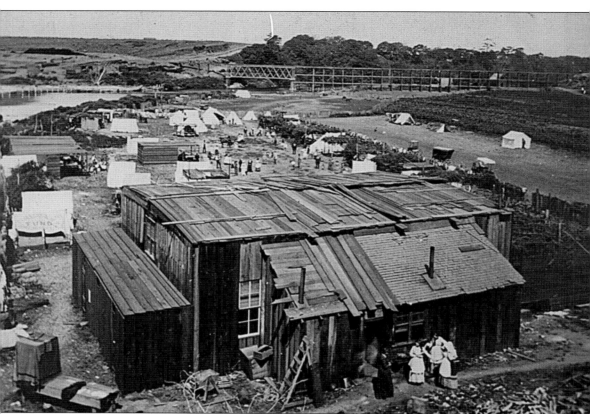

When Michael Lodge and Martina Castro Lodge left Capitola for gold mining country in 1848, they abandoned a profitable potato crop. A few years later, the alluvial flat was still planted in spuds, spurred by the demands of hungry miners. The earliest known structure in today's Capitola Village was a potato warehouse built in 1851. But when the demand abruptly ceased, the shoreline was heaped with surplus, rotting potatoes. New crops were planted after Frederick Hihn bought the 2-mile stretch between Soquel Creek and Borregas Gulch in 1856. Hihn leased the flat to Soquel farmer Samuel Alonzo Hall in 1869. This 1876 image shows the freshly established Camp Capitola campground on the left and Hall's agricultural fields at the far right. (Courtesy of the Capitola Historical Museum.)

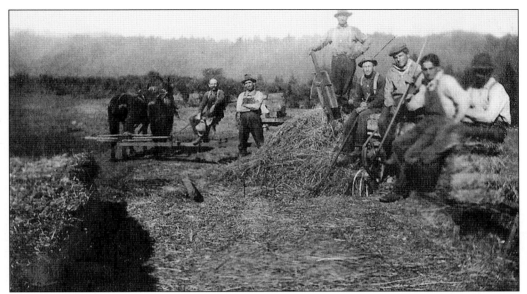

Once the redwood trees had been logged from the hills and their stumps cleared, agriculture moved into the mountains. William R. Jones is pictured here sitting on a hay baler powered by the team, while his brother-in-law, Clyde Iliff, rests on the hay, fourth from the right. The baled hay was stored in a barn and used for livestock feed in the winter months. (Courtesy of the William R. Jones family.)

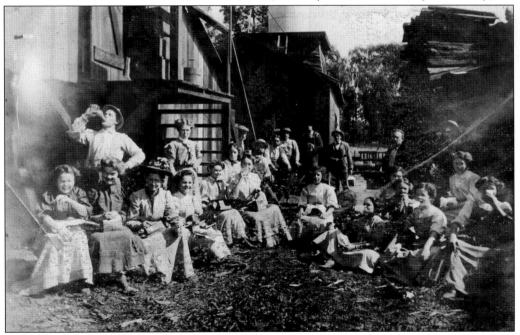

A crew enjoys a break about 1912 at the apple dryer and vinegar works owned by Soquel native Olley Richard Nutter (1882–1941). The operation at Capitola Avenue and Hill Street was rebuilt after a fire in the early 1920s and expanded to become the Nutter and Russell Apple Dryer and Vinegar Plant. More than 75 workers from Soquel and Capitola were employed in the busy periods. (Courtesy of Richard Nutter.)

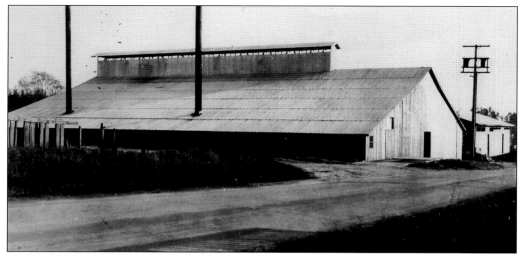

Fresh local apples were processed for cider, vinegar, and dried apple products at the Nutter and Russell plant. Fruit was processed by placing apples in a mechanical peeler that also removed the core. They were then sliced, dusted with sulfur, dried, and shipped throughout the nation. An estimated 500,000 gallons of vinegar were held in tanks on the premises. (Courtesy of Richard Nutter.)

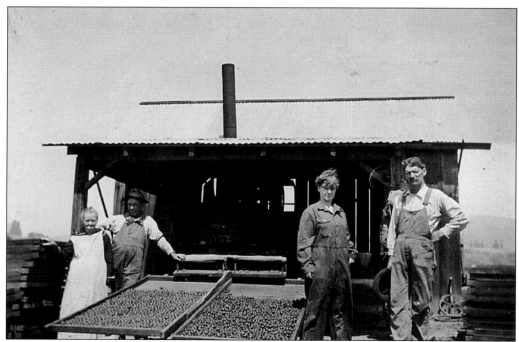

Large acreages of prunes dotted Soquel hills until the 1950s. This European plum variety required no irrigation and little maintenance and grew on hilly terrain. The fruit was dried and sold nationally. Harvesting required many workers to shake the trees and pick up the prunes. They were placed in trays and put in a homemade dryer, as shown in this Don Emery ranch photograph. (Courtesy of Horton Kooser.)

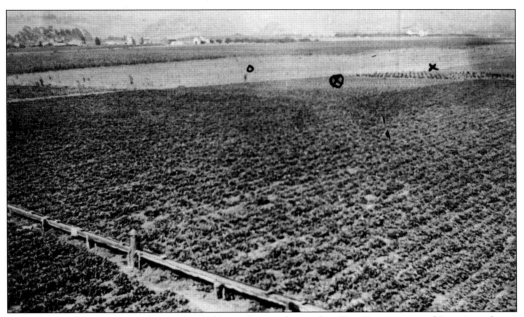

Strawberries became popular in the 1920s and were shipped to San Francisco and Los Angeles as well as to local markets. Level land was needed to meet irrigation requirements. In this photograph, a wooded irrigation flume runs diagonally across the lower portion of the field along Forty-first Avenue, bordering Soquel and Capitola. (Courtesy of the James Brown family and Brown Ranch Market Place.)

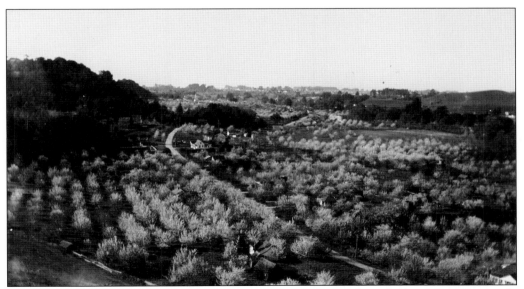

Soquel was an important cherry growing region from the 1860s through the 1950s. Cherryvale Avenue, pictured above and looking south toward the ocean, was an exceptionally productive district. In one week during the 1930s, more than 32,000 pounds were produced from these orchards. The cherries were shipped to markets in San Francisco and Los Angeles. (Courtesy of the William R. Jones family.)

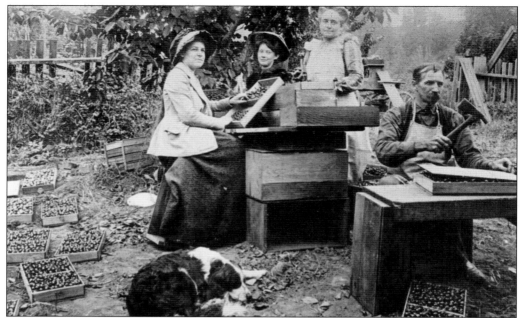

Soquel pioneer Joshua Parrish introduced cherries to the Soquel Valley. The Wymans, relatives of the Parrish family, were busy picking and packing Black Tartarian cherries at Fred Wyman's orchard in Soquel when this photograph was taken about 1908. Pictured from left to right are Laura (Wyman) Maddock, Ethel Hudson, Annie Wyman, and Fred Wyman. Rover's job was to provide good company.

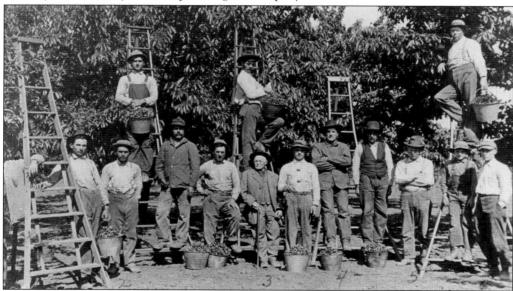

Augustus Noble, standing with his cane, center, celebrates with his cherry-picking crew on one spectacularly productive day in 1913. Paul Johnston, far right, recorded the event on his copy of the photograph. The Noble orchard yielded 3,420 pounds of cherries that day. The fruit was packed in 114 boxes and loaded on a wagon for shipment to Los Angeles. (Courtesy of the Museum of Art and History.)

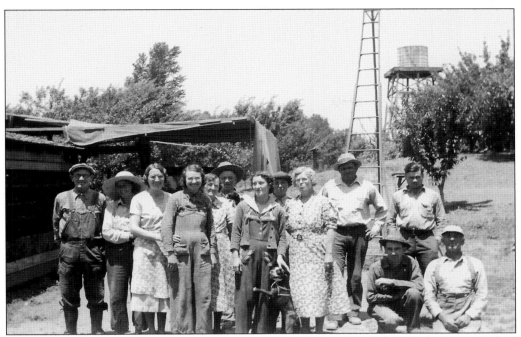

Picking cherries was labor intensive. Each fruit was picked by hand and placed in buckets and then sorted for market. Soquel picking crews pose above and below during work breaks in the 1930s. The very tall ladder in the background above was used for harvesting. The tank house supplied water for domestic purposes and orchard irrigation. Many of the pickers had come to California from the Midwest during the Great Depression, and they were paid by the number of pounds harvested. (Above, courtesy of the William R. Jones family; below, courtesy of the Hazel Bardt family.)

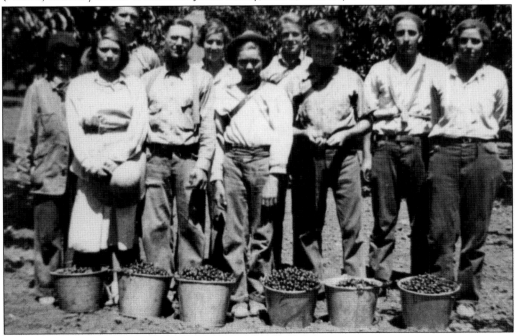

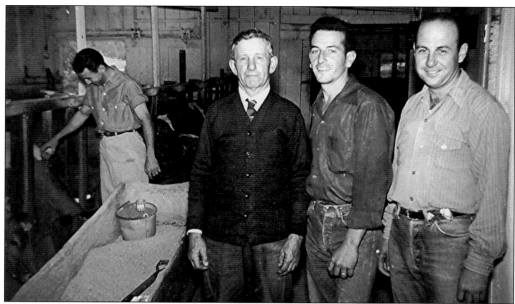

Morris Negro emigrated from Italy in 1901, eventually settling near Soquel in Live Oak, where he ran a chicken ranch. He later admitted that he did not even know how to milk a cow when he decided to start up a dairy on 12 acres he bought along Soquel San Jose Road. He established the Valley View Dairy about 1938, expanding it to 208 acres with 160 cows, hay and milking barns, four houses, and a pasteurizing plant. Pictured above in the milking barn are, from left to right, son Ernest Negro, father Morris Negro, employee Joe Santos, and son Ray Negro. Morris ran the plant until his death in 1952, and his wife, Lucy, continued to operate it for several years with their sons. Grandchildren Loretta and Kenneth Negro enjoyed playing around the barn and are pictured below introducing their puppy to the cows. (Both, courtesy of the Negro family.)

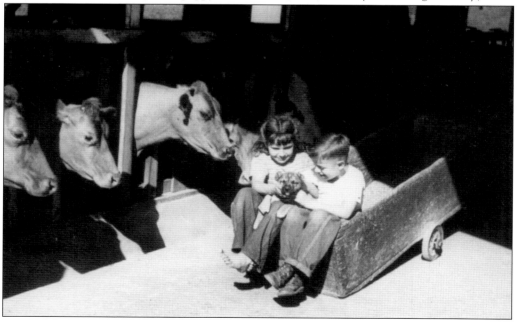

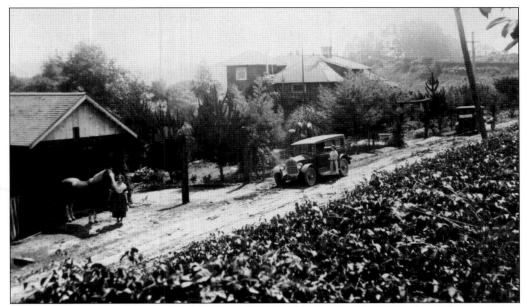

Edith Pawla of Pawla's Violet Gardens on Wharf Road was one of few specialty violet growers in the nation. In 1917, she and daughter Emily purchased the Frank Daubenbiss home. Collecting over 100 violet varieties, they sold plants by mail-order catalog. Edith was later recognized as the hybridizer of the *Viola odorata* "Royal Robe." The International Violet Society honored the Pawlas for contributions to the industry. (Courtesy of Shirley Coleman.)

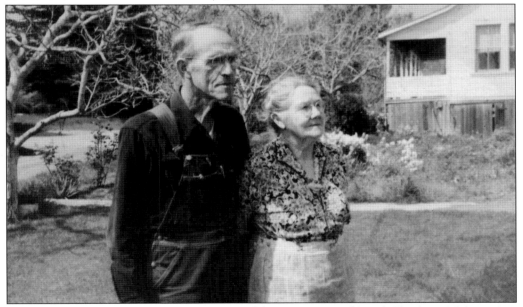

Settling into an older house near Porter Gulch in 1921, Harold and Charlotte Nelson were familiar with farm life. They had eight children, raised chickens, and grew calla lilies. The couple is remembered for their service to Soquel as founders of the Soquel 4-H Club, and they guided its young members for 30 years. Both Harold and Charlotte were also active with the Farm Bureau. (Courtesy of the Nelson family.)

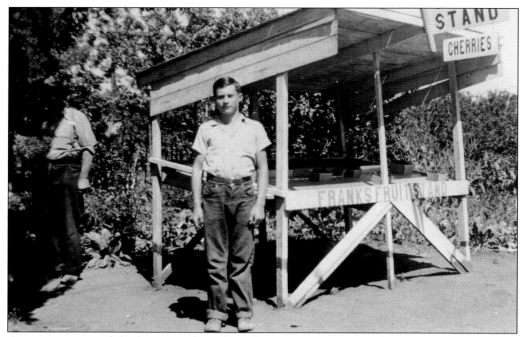

As soon as automobiles began rattling along Santa Cruz County roadways, fruit and vegetable stands sprouted everywhere. Joe and Pierina Beccaria and son Frank owned one along Bay Avenue, selling fruit from their nearby orchards. Frank is standing at front in this 1939 photograph, taken a decade before new road construction cut through, leaving the Beccaria stand by an off-ramp on the Capitola side of Highway 1. (Courtesy of Frank Beccaria.)

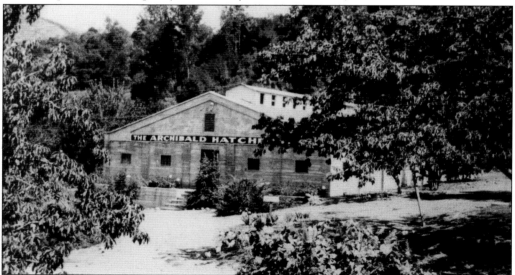

Chicken and egg production became a profitable Soquel industry in the early 1900s. Small ranches raised a few thousand chickens each. The ranchers, in turn, sold their eggs to a cooperative that distributed to retail outlets. Archibald Hatchery, located on Cherryvale Avenue, hatched over 200,000 chicks annually and sold the pullets (female chicks) to area farmers. It had the capacity to hatch 60,000 chicks at a time.

Four

BUSINESS
HARDWARE TO HAIRCUTS

Soquel Creek zigzags through the heart of the village as it winds its way from the mountains to the bay. Because the meandering path demands more bridges than one would expect in a town of Soquel's size, transportation strongly influenced where the business district began and how it grew.

Until 1886, nothing but a planked pedestrian span called a "summer bridge" existed on Soquel Drive. Instead, coaches and freight were diverted to two permanent crossings, one at Bridge Street and one at Walnut Street. Built in 1867, these were the "upper and lower" bridges, guiding passage through town in an H-shaped pattern. This traffic configuration lasted roughly 35 years, with commercial markets and shops clustered at the corners leading off the main road. Orchards and vacant lots were in between.

Once a steel bridge crossed the creek at Soquel Drive, traffic routes adjusted. By the time the Walnut Street Bridge collapsed in 1912 and the link at Bridge Street fell in 1928, people were already beginning to wonder why Main Street had that name. When the automobile arrived, cars driving back and forth between Santa Cruz and Aptos could power through the Soquel Drive intersections and straight up the hills on either side. The Porter Street connection remained a crucial junction, as it is today, but over the years, the businesses have slowly become isolated as the streets are congested with rush-hour traffic.

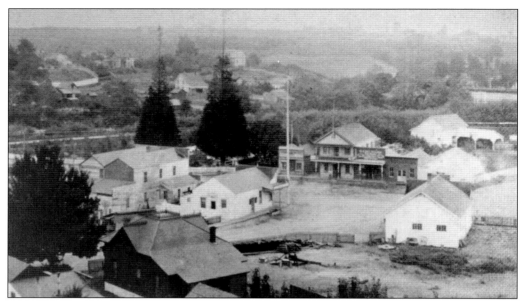

In 1856, David Brownstone founded Soquel's earliest store. Ned Porter bought it a year later. The business, located on Soquel Drive near the Porter Street intersection, also housed the first post office, established July 5, 1857. J. T. Harlan acquired the store in 1883, selling it a few years later to Fenner A. Angell. Angell first operated it with his brother Horatio. The store is the two-story building shown at center right about 1895.

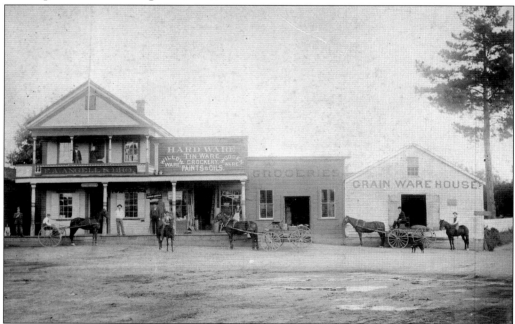

Fenner Angell and his wife, Margaret, stand on the second-floor balcony of their store about 1890. William "Billy the Barber" Kropf is at far left, near his barbershop. The Angells' business extended to the corner of Porter Street, where a new market was built by son Clarence in 1932. The family also leased the seasonal store concession at Camp Capitola during its early years.

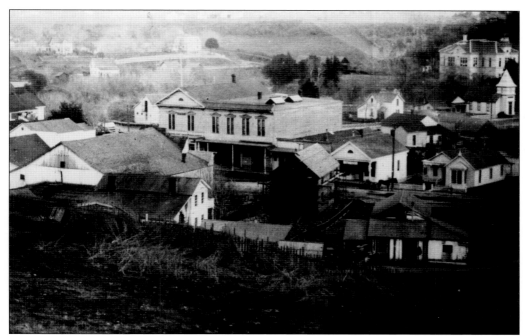

Photographed from the O'Neill ranch, about 1892, the view above shows commercial buildings near the Porter Street intersection. The IOOF (Independent Order of Odd Fellows) Hall is in the center. Soquel Grammar School is in the upper right corner. The school is to the far left in the picture below, taken about the same time. A gristmill and the Park House Hotel are at the center along Porter Street. The IOOF Hall and a string of shops are in the foreground. Daubenbiss Street, at far right, connects to Soquel Drive. Barely visible near the trees along the coast is a remnant from the 1870s beet sugar mill. It was described on the photograph as an old yellow warehouse used to store potatoes.

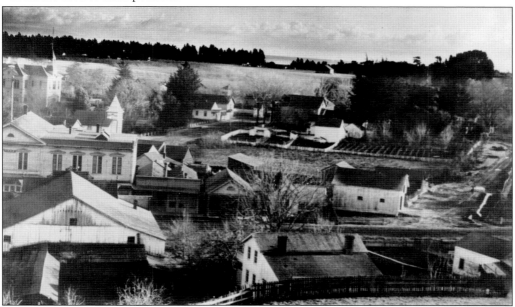

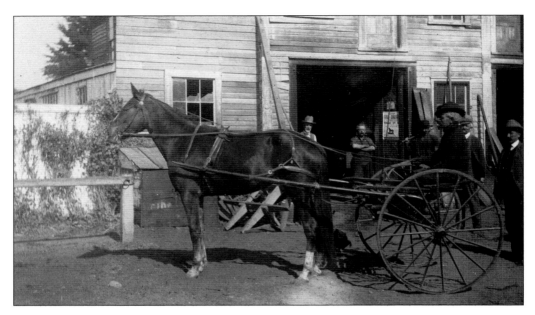

The 1858 hotel built by A. F. Bryant and Peter Canares on the north side of Soquel Drive near Porter Street also served a government function. Lambert Clements, justice of the peace, held court in a room off the bar. Stagecoach driver Charley Parkhurst voted here in the 1868 presidential election. When the tobacco-chewing, foul-mouthed "Cockeyed Charley" died in 1879, friends discovered suspicions were true—their longtime pal was actually a woman. The place she voted eventually became Mann's Hotel, run by Abel Mann and his son, Tom. Converted into the Mason and Schellenger blacksmith shop about 1895, it is shown above around 1898 with wheelwright Charles Mason, far right; Clarence Schellenger, the blacksmith, at the right side of the doorway; and Billy Nash, the driver. Benjamin Parrish, in the buggy, poses below with the owners.

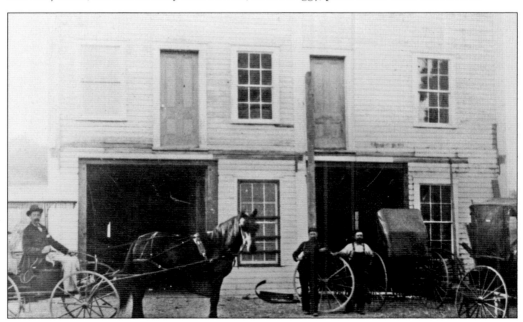

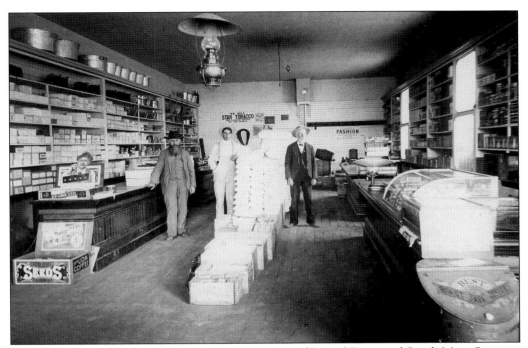

Ozro M. Ellis opened his hardware store at the corner of Soquel Drive and South Main Street in 1887. The inventory changed to general merchandise at the time this photograph was taken in the mid-1890s. Ellis and his son, Leslie L., are standing with a neighbor, Soquel School principal W. R. Wilson. A fire later destroyed the building.

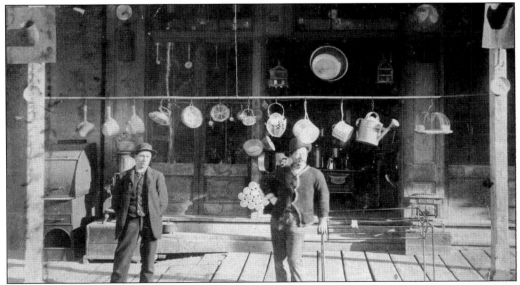

At age 17, Isaac Fleisig left his native Austria for the United States. A decade later, he was the father of four children and proprietor of a mercantile store located in the IOOF building in downtown Soquel. A pioneer dealer in general merchandise, wines, and liquors, Fleisig sold everything from pots and pans to birdcages and watering cans. This picture outside the store was taken about 1885.

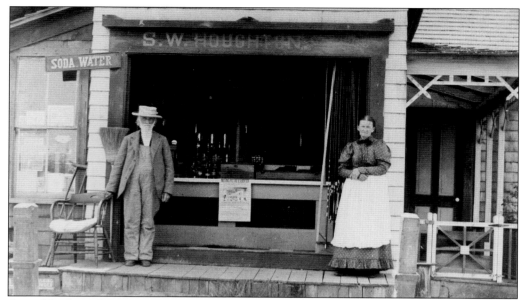

One of the Soquel stores outside the village was operated in the 1890s by Solon Whiting Houghton and his wife, Evelyn (Everlin) Houghton. The little market at the southwest corner of Soquel Drive and Monterey Avenue was in a neighborhood known as "Hardscrabble." This photograph was taken about 1895.

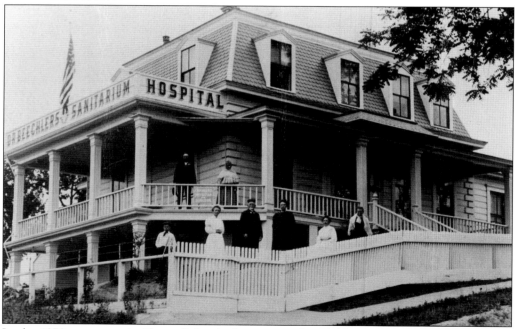

In the 1870s, sea captain Henry Baker built a mansard-roofed home at South Main and East Walnut Streets. His daughter, Matilda Baker, was a longtime Soquel School teacher. The house sold to veteran Civil War surgeon Dr. James Beechler, who established a sanitarium hospital. After he retired, the buildings were bought by E. S. Yantis, who converted them into an apartment complex. In 1934, a fire gutted all but a few remaining outbuildings.

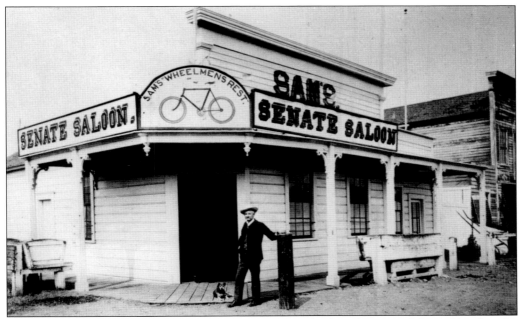

Sam Alkire of Sam's Senate Saloon took advantage of the bicycle craze of the 1890s when he identified his tavern as "Sam's Wheelmen's Rest." The saloon, at the northeast corner of Soquel Drive and Porter Street, was a popular stop for tired and thirsty teamsters. Later, as automobile traffic increased through town, it was the site of Lloyd Pringle's X-Ray Garage.

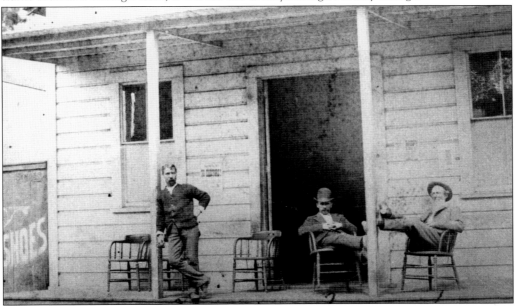

James Fitzjames Bennett (1819–1891), right, arrived in the 1850s and married Jane Rice, a daughter of Judge Henry Rice. Bennett operated several flour mills and also served as county clerk, auditor, and superintendent of schools. He managed the former Hames and Daubenbiss mill on Porter Street. Nearby, he built a hotel. After it burned, Bennett opened a saloon. His companions are Billy Williams, center, and Billy Chatterson, left.

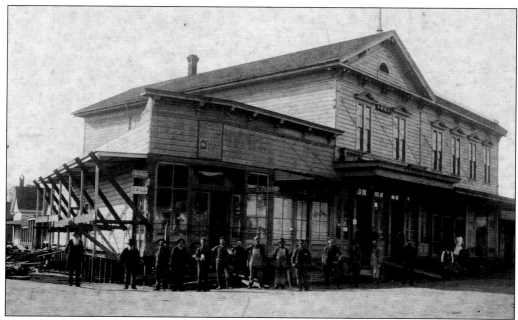

Loren T. Hill and his wife, Sarah, moved to Soquel before 1880 and, with their son, Henry, opened a grocery store on an irregular, pie-shaped lot at the corner of Porter Street, next to the IOOF Hall. The store was owned later by Edgar D. Webb and then James T. Lowry, who purchased it with Jarvis Esty. The original structure was replaced in the 1930s by a streamlined stucco building.

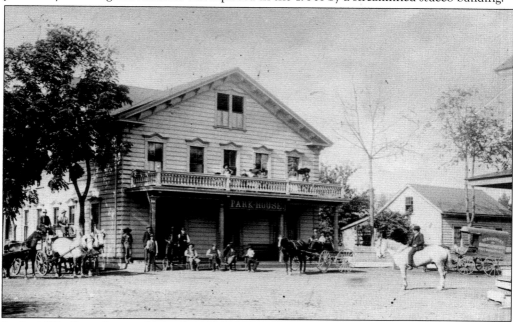

In the 1850s, Peter Canares built a hostelry at West Walnut and Porter Streets. It was conveniently located along the route from Soquel to the wharf at the coastline. Alexander Getzschmann (on horse) bought the hotel in the 1860s and renamed it the Park House. It was replaced by a larger structure in 1885. The building was renovated and reopened as the Soquel Inn in 1945.

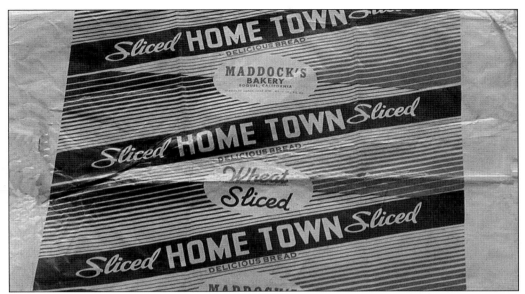

Maddock's Bakery is remembered for its pastries and breads. Harold Maddock bought it in the mid-1930s and operated the bakery until he sold it to another owner in 1952. On holidays, Maddock took in turkeys and baked them for his neighbors. He also made starter bread for customers to finish at home. The 1940s wrapper above is from the time when Maddock made deliveries to local markets. (Courtesy of Ted Maddock.)

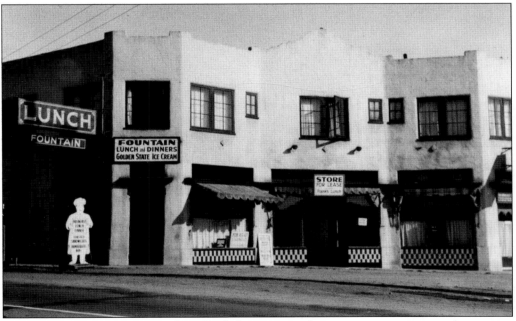

Frank Kasseroller, an immigrant from Tyrol, Austria, was a longtime concessionaire and restaurant owner at Capitola. Moving to Soquel in the mid-1930s, he designed the structure above with a fountain and offices on the ground floor and apartments on the second floor. Today the building houses antique shops at Soquel Drive and South Main Street. (Courtesy of the Museum of Art and History.)

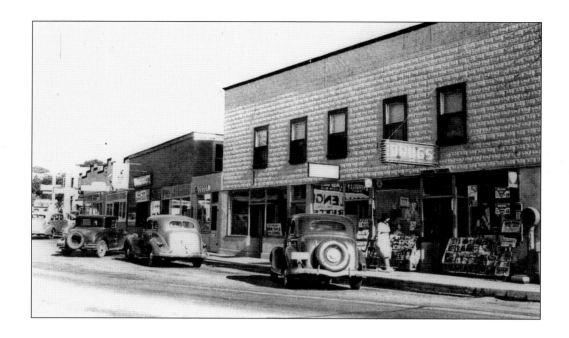

The corner of Main Street and Soquel Drive began to develop commercially once the 1886 bridge was built. A cluster of early stores was replaced in 1925 with a string of modern structures owned by Lewis Dingwall. W. O. Rushton's grocery, Al Buck's Soquel Hardware Store, Bill Finta's Soquel Pharmacy, a butcher, a barber, and a dress shop all burned along with the Dingwall Apartments in 1940.

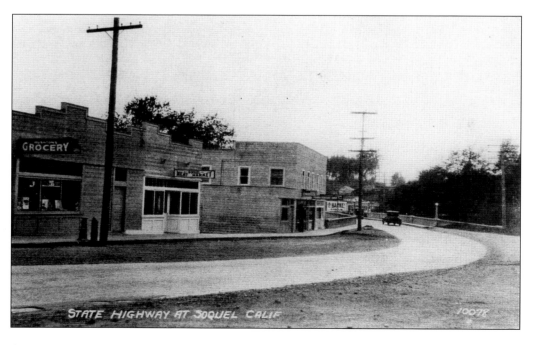

Five

SOQUELITES
LEAVING LASTING IMPRESSIONS

It is easy to tell who left a lasting impression in Soquel. Their names are lettered on directional signs and sprinkled over maps. They mark the landscape—a creek, grove, hill, and gulch or a building, a bridge, or a roadway. The imprints of pioneers are solidly linked to landmarks of wood, concrete, and earth. Other traces, less visible, are stored in historical records. These are stamped into documents, penciled on the backs of photographs, or told in legends until they are cast into community memory as solidly as rock.

Soquel has a Noble Gulch, Bates Creek, Pringle Grove, Parrish Hill, Porter Street, and Littlejohn Bridge. Stories and biographies of community-spirited Soquelites are glued into scrapbooks that grow shabbier each year from thumbing and scrutiny at annual picnics. Former classmates still swap memories of such revered teachers as Kate Leonard, Marion Kevil, and Alice Woolsey.

Soquel's character has been shaped by immigrant settlers who broadened the town's character as they quickly adapted to differing customs and points of view. They came in number from Germany, Italy, Ireland, Portugal, Russia, China, and Japan. Each group has its own story.

In the 1880s, John Costella—nicknamed "Garibaldi" for his time with the army in Italy—worked in Grover's sawmill for 11 years before deciding to make a trip back home. He returned with 13 others, including Delfina, his bride. Pasquallo Battagliola and Antonio Bergazzi from the Apennine Mountains were among the new arrivals. Later, mill workers Frank Speroni and Bartolomeo Bertorelli brought over their families to join them.

Costella left Soquel in 1885 and eventually built the famed Garibaldi Villa Hotel in Santa Cruz. He remained, however, supportive of Soquel's Italian community. Families that he brought to Grover's Gulch established farms that were productive long after the mills ran out of timber. Among names still familiar in the region are Locatelli, Brida, Rebuffo, and Tola.

Township residents were diverse in their countries of origin, ways of thinking, and methods of work. Often arriving as foreigners and strangers, they fit themselves in, held fast in their surroundings, and built a community.

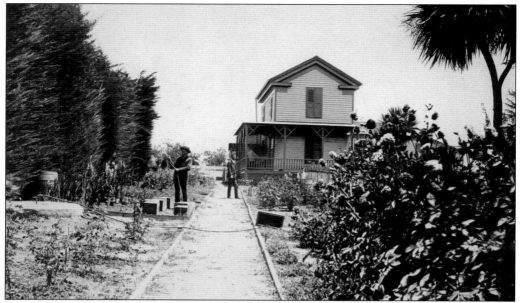

Augustus Noble (1823–1915) sailed from New England to California during the Gold Rush, settling near Sacramento. In 1856, he bought 120 Soquel acres that included the Castro-Lodge adobe. Noble built a home next door (above, *c.* 1910) on present-day Hill Street, now in Capitola. He planted apple and cherry orchards, was envied for his flowers, and created a subdivision called Rosedale. (Courtesy of Richard Nutter.)

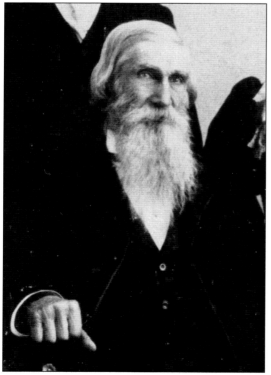

Wagon train scout Joshua Parrish (1815–1898) rode from Ohio to California as a forty-niner. He bought a tract in Soquel from Carmel and Thomas Fallon and bred horses. His crops of potatoes and grain sold well at the mines, allowing Parrish to go back to Ohio in 1853 to marry Narcissa Dell. He returned to Soquel with fruit trees and planted orchards throughout the valley. (Courtesy of Ted Maddock.)

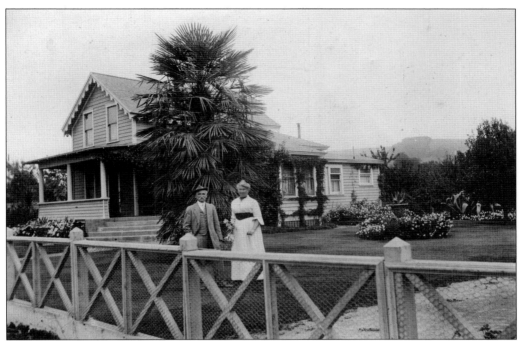

William "Billy the Barber" Kropf (1853–1923) migrated from New York in the 1870s with his German-born parents, William J. and Anna R. Kropf. He became one of Soquel's first barbers. Married in 1895, Billy and his wife, Frances, posed years later outside their Porter Street home. When he died in 1923, his red-and-white-striped barbershop poles were used on the outside stairs to Frances's residence.

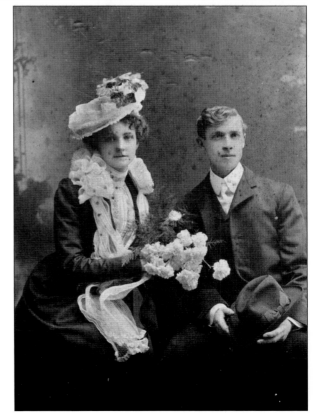

Lloyd Sturtevant Pringle (1876–1948) was a descendant of the pioneer Pringle and Anthony families of Santa Cruz. He opened Shannon and Pringle's X-Ray Garage, an automobile repair shop, and also served many years as Soquel's postmaster. In the mid-1940s, Pringle and his wife, the former Anne E. Maddock, donated to the Soquel Pioneer and Historical Association a wooded setting known as Pringle Grove. (Courtesy of the Pringle family.)

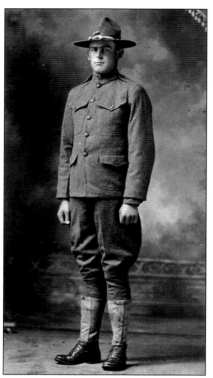

Fay Wyman, 26, son of Addi W. and Anna J. Wyman and grandson of Joshua and Narcissa Parrish, died in 1918 following the Battle of Argonne in France. An officer was cleaning his rifle nearby when it exploded, killing Wyman. He was the only Soquel soldier who died overseas in World War I. The Fay Wyman Post of the Veterans of Foreign Wars was named in his honor. He is buried at Arlington Cemetery. (Courtesy of Ted Maddock.)

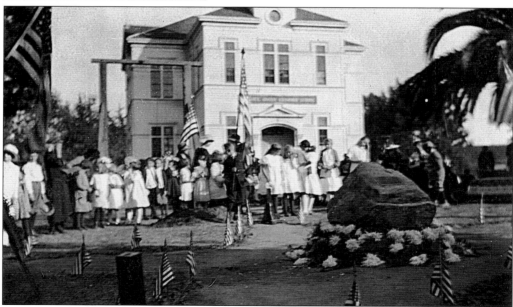

On Armistice Day, 1923, a memorial was dedicated at Soquel School honoring Wyman and Evan Marlin of Capitola, who died at training camp as the war ended. Nora Angell and Lloyd Bowman found the perfect granite boulder in what is today Henry Cowell Redwoods State Park. Now standing tall are the redwood trees planted to form a five-pointed star around the memorial. (Courtesy of Ted Maddock.)

A wildfire swept across the timbered Santa Cruz Mountains above Soquel on October 8, 1899. Ernst Emil Meyer, owner of Mare Vista Winery, and his son battled the blaze. When it swept upon the ranch, Yeng Ah, the family's Chinese cook, without orders, collected containers and pulled together a brigade of workers to save the Meyer home. They succeeded. When efforts failed to slow flames advancing on the winery, Meyer's son attached a hose to the wine vats and used 4,000 gallons of claret to douse the flames. The cook's unselfish efforts were recorded later in a magazine article, and for more than a century, photographs of the 24-year-old hero, shown right and below, have been kept by the family. (Both, courtesy of Joel Muckleroy and the Meyer-Matty family.)

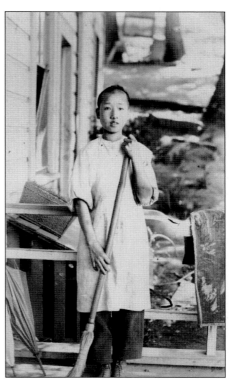

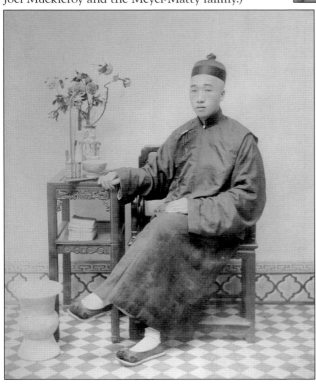

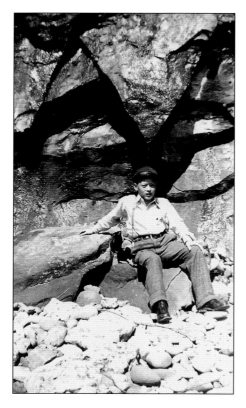

Joe Seta, a young Japanese, lived and worked on William R. Jones's orchard on Cherryvale Avenue off Main Street. He was interned in Arizona when World War II started, and there he met and married Sofia, a Native American. Her photograph was sent back to the Jones family in Soquel in 1944. The couple's whereabouts after the war are unknown. Seta had been among a number of Japanese living in Soquel, including the Masamori and Kishimoto families. All were sent to western internment camps in 1942. Some of the younger Masamoris returned to Soquel, but the Kishimotos and Seta never came back. (Courtesy of the William R. Jones family.)

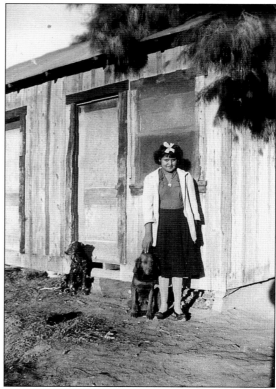

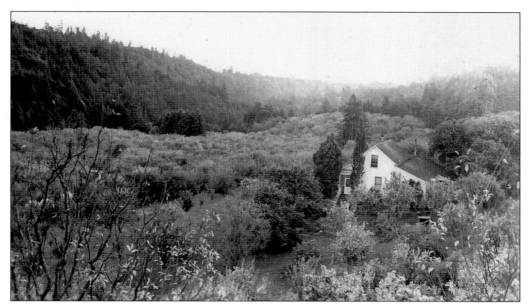

Two brothers of the Manildi family emigrated from the Piedmonte region of Italy in the 1880s, choosing Soquel for its scenery and climate that were suggestive of home. Jack (Secondo) Manildi, 16, joined his brothers here in 1890. Soon he co-owned a vegetable farm in the growing Italian region of Soquel. In 1904, Jack married Sadie Garaventa and settled on Glen Haven Road in the former summer home of sawmill owner Lyman Grover. Jack enhanced his "stump farm" by clearing the land and planting orchards. The family home is shown about 1930. The c. 1920 portrait includes Albert, the eldest child, seated far left. He managed the farm after the death of his father and helped to raise his youngest brothers and sister. (Both, courtesy of the Manildi family.)

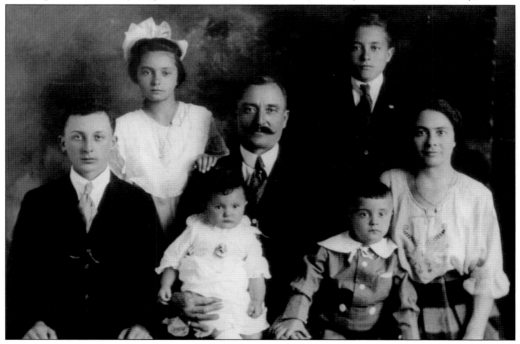

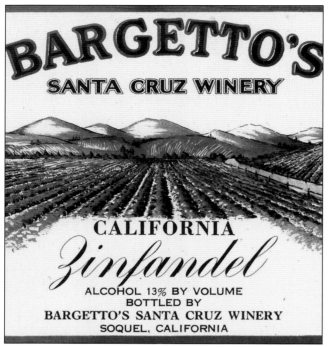

BARGETTO'S

SANTA CRUZ WINERY

CALIFORNIA

Zinfandel

ALCOHOL 13% BY VOLUME
BOTTLED BY
BARGETTO'S SANTA CRUZ WINERY
SOQUEL, CALIFORNIA

Brothers Phillip and John Bargetto came from Castelnuovo Don Bosco in Italy's Piedmonte region, the homeland of many Italian immigrants to Soquel. Phillip left Italy in 1891 at the age of 17, followed by John in 1909. The brothers arrived with vast winegrowing experience, establishing the original Bargetto Winery in San Francisco. In 1917, they closed it and moved to Soquel. Unable to create wine for sale during Prohibition, they made it for family and friends while growing apples and produce for local customers. John's son Lawrence took charge of production during the 1960s and 1970s and pioneered new techniques. A third generation now directs the business. (Both, courtesy of the Bargetto family.)

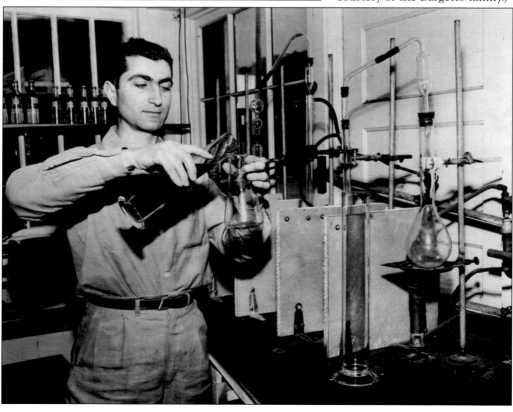

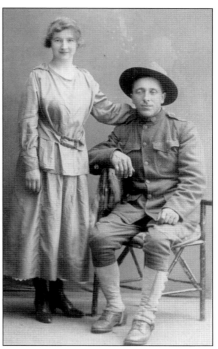

Antonio and Madelena Ponza were both from San Michele in the Piedmonte district. The Ponza brothers—Lorenzo, George, and Antonio, the youngest—came to California in the early 1900s. Initially, they contracted in the Glenwood timber industry, making split stuff. The 1919 photograph at right was taken following Antonio's U.S. Army infantry service in World War I. The couple raised four children at their ranch off Rodeo Gulch Road in Soquel. Antonio's son Michael and two of the Oneto brothers point toward the family cherry orchards and vineyard in the photograph below. (Both, courtesy of the Ponza family.)

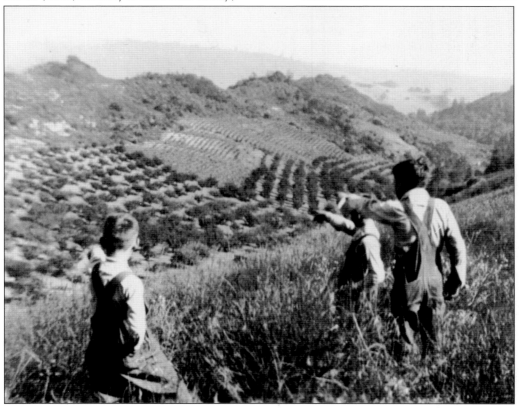

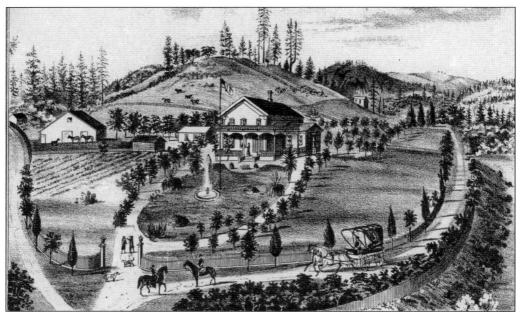

George Casalegno was among those who came from Italy's Piedmonte district in the early 1900s. Vera Cisi, born in San Francisco in 1898, moved to Soquel as a child, met George in 1915, and married him a year later. The couple raised four sons and two daughters in their home on the former Benjamin Cahoon Ranch (above), located at the junction of Soquel San Jose Road and Laurel Glen Road. The Casalegnos built a store where they sold groceries, homegrown produce, and gasoline. Frank Casalegno, a son, was partially paralyzed from an injury in 1938, but he managed the store from his wheelchair. In the 1948 store photograph, Frank fills the radiator of brother Bill's 1926 Model T. The Cahoon ranch lithograph above is from W. W. Elliott's *Santa Cruz County, California, Illustrations, with Historical Sketch*, 1879. (Above, courtesy of the Capitola Historical Museum; below, courtesy of the Casalegno family.)

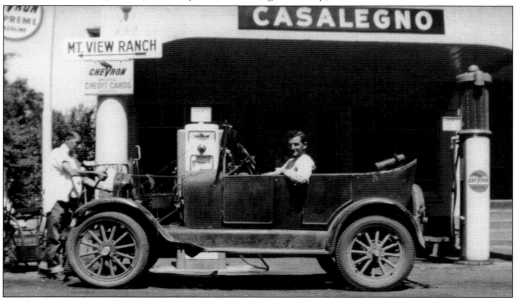

Flatfish was the catch of the day for Hettie and Rudolph Getzschmann, center, posing with Edward O'Neill, right, on Wharf Road in Capitola about 1910. Max Schmidt, fishing excursion boat operator, is on the left. Rudolph's parents, Alex and Agnes Getzschmann, migrated from Germany and settled in Soquel about 1865. Alex ran a gristmill on today's Daubenbiss Avenue, owned the Park House Hotel on Porter Street, and was a builder of the South Coast Paper Mill. Below, twins Ed (left)and John (right), sons of Rudolph and Hettie, are waiting with relatives at the Union Traction Company streetcar terminus at Capitola in 1924. (Both, courtesy of John Getzschmann.)

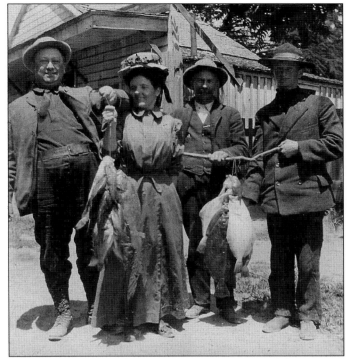

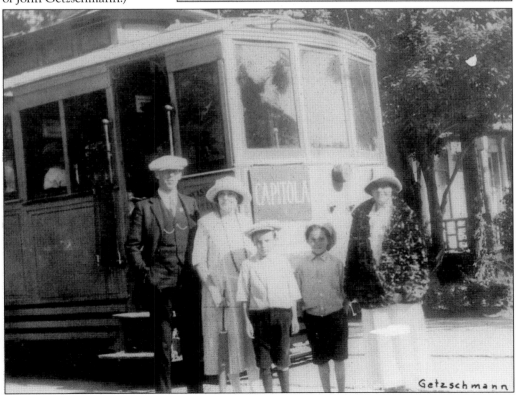

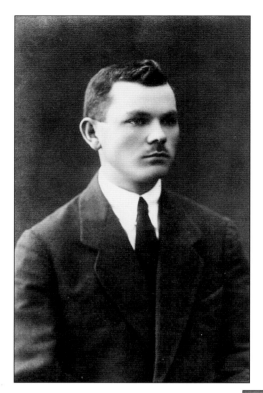

In 1925, two Russian refugees from the Revolution of 1917, both from agriculture backgrounds, bought a small acreage from the Prescott family on Glen Haven Road. They were two of several Russians who settled in or near Soquel. Ivan "John" Harlamoff, left, and Alexei "Alec" Temerin, below, established a chicken business. Harlamoff also worked part-time at Prescott's Inn and was a friend of Tom Prescott, who introduced him to Ethel Jones. The couple married in 1928 and established a family chicken farm along Soquel San Jose Road. The Harlamoff-Prescott friendship lasted their lifetimes. Harlamoff was active in the Soquel community, helping with local war efforts during World War II and serving as a 4-H leader. He died in 1990 at almost 92 years of age. (Both, courtesy of the Harlamoff family.)

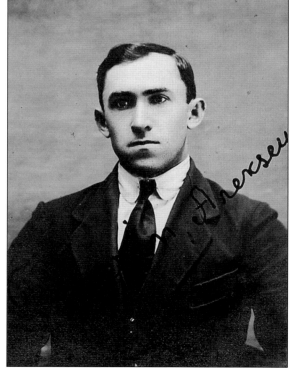

Six

OUR TOWN
BUILDING COMMUNITY

Addressing the Soquel Pioneer and Historical Association at its 70th annual picnic in 2008, historian Sandy Lydon asked what Soquel residents like to be called. Were they Soquelis, Soquelians, Soquelites, or—as Lydon tendered—Soquelistas?

The majority declared themselves Soquelites, a name often cited in old newspapers. Soquelistas still got enough approval to credit the town's initial scrappy nature back in 1852.

After the Gold Rush, Soquel was built with a spirited vigor. Booming industry called for the hasty construction of saloons, stores, hotels, and blacksmith shops, followed by churches, schools, and social halls, as well as a neatly plotted cemetery. But the heartiness gradually diminished as fortunes shifted, manufacturing slowed, and the landscape was altered.

Local news reporter Laura Rawson, writing in 1932, summarized the downturn. "The humming busyness of the seventies and eighties in Soquel lent it an importance which subsequent growth has never again matched," she said.

Soquel matured with an agrarian economy, and residents adapted with a down-to-earth sensibility. The gumption was there but showed up less often, usually in "do-or-die" moments that spurred a call to action.

The fate of the Soquel Porter Memorial Library tells the story. Built on land donated by William T. and Mary Sesnon, the library's 1912 construction was the joint effort of Porter family descendants and the Ladies of the Soquel Improvement Society, led by Nora (Oliver) Angell. For 66 years, the institution remained a source of pride—for the cultural life it gave the town, for its architecture, and for its endurance in the face of disaster. But suddenly in the summer of 1978, the Soquel branch was ordered closed.

Stepping in, Mona and Bob Blankholm rallied support that has continued to keep the library open for more than 30 years, creating "the little library that could."

Volunteers mustered to repair damages after the 1982 flood and the 1989 Loma Prieta earthquake. In 2008, the Bargetto family, celebrating their winery's 75th anniversary, financed a renovation of the library's exterior. The structure's revived appearance fits its stature as a landmark designed by master architects.

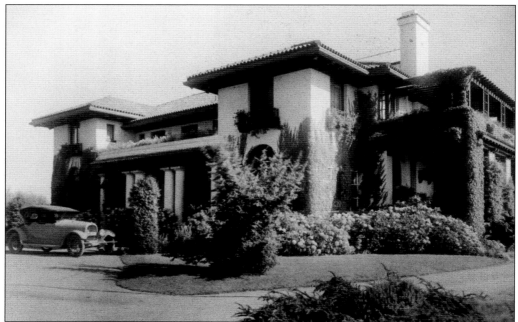

Mary Sophia Porter Sesnon, daughter of Benjamin and Catherine Porter, and her husband, William T. Sesnon of San Francisco, were ready in 1911 to move into their new country home on the site of the family estate. As they did so, the couple was approached by Soquel townspeople, who asked for help to create a library. To honor Mary's parents, the Sesnons donated the Porter Street lot, matched the funds raised, and provided their architects, Clarence R. Ward and J. H. Blohme, to design the $3,000 Mission Revival–style building. The grand opening was January 28, 1913. Pictured above is the Sesnon Mansion, described by journalists as a structure "harkening back to aristocratic old Spain." Ward and Blohme took a similar—although far more modest—approach to the Soquel Library's architecture. The branch is under construction during the 1912 community event shown below. (Above, courtesy of the Porter Sesnon family.)

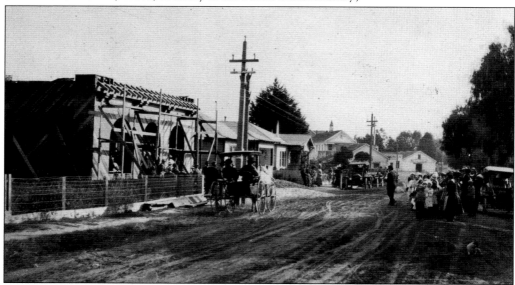

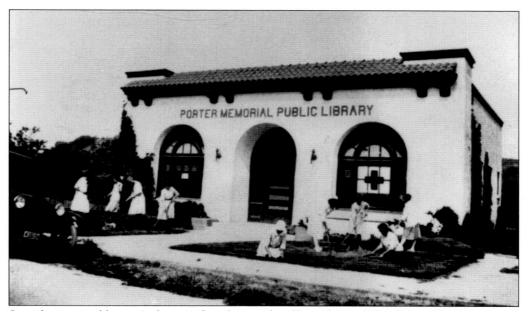

Soquel reveres its library. A plaque in front honors the efforts of Nora (Oliver) Angell and the Soquel Improvement Society. Shown are gardening Campfire Girls, from left to right, (kneeling) Marion (Nutter) Ross and Ceedola (Parrish) Duff; (standing) Thelma (Ryder) Sylva, Ruth (Archibald) McGhee, Alice Chegindden, Elaine Welty, Gladys Peters, Olive Welty, and Beatrice Hensel. A World War I–era Red Cross banner is in the window. (Courtesy Ruth Archibald McGhee.)

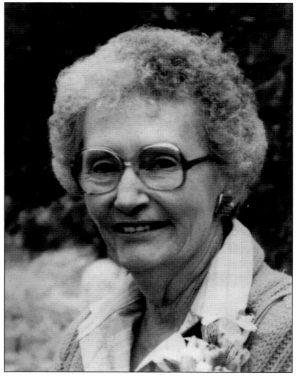

Mona Blankholm approached the board of supervisors in 1978 with a deed to prove that Mary Porter Sesnon conveyed the library building and land to the county "for the purpose of erecting and maintaining thereon a free public library for the use of the residents in and about Soquel in said County." The building, although still county-owned, is occupied rent free and maintained by the Soquel Porter Memorial Library Board of Directors.

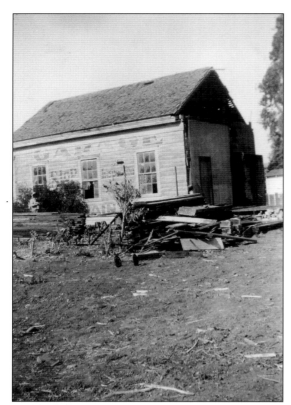

Soquel's founders each built schools in the 1850s. John Hames constructed one on Porter Street opposite Paper Mill Road, while John Daubenbiss built another below his own house. A larger school, pictured, was located in the late 1860s on the west side of Porter Street. Nellie and Frank Holdaway demolished it in 1940, building a home with the lumber. It was razed in the 1990s. (Courtesy of Jolene Nicklanovich.)

In 1871, the *Santa Cruz Sentinel* reported "Soquel is noted for more children than any town of its size in the State." The village had separate schools for primary, intermediate, and grammar grades. The smaller schools were combined when the two-story school below was completed in 1890. Pioneer Santa Cruz County educator John W. Linscott (1848–1931) and his wife, Emma, pose in front of the school.

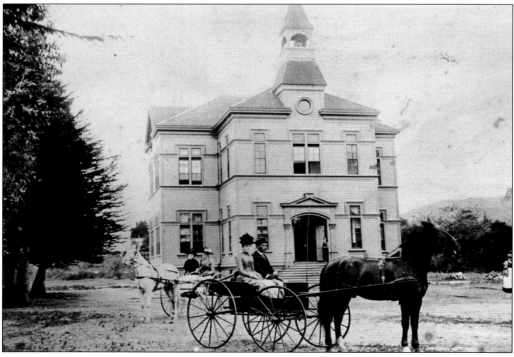

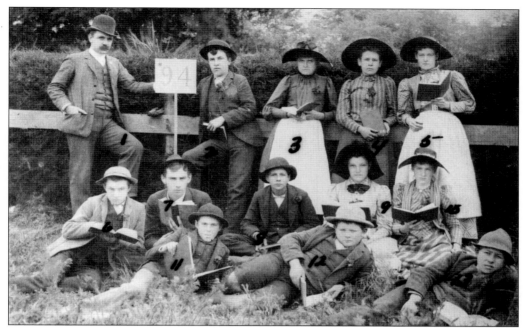

The 1894 Soquel School graduating class relaxes for an outdoor portrait with their principal, William E. Dodge. From left to right are (seated) Horace Mason, John Casey, Charles Bostwick, George Fleckner, Harry Martin, Cara Golightly, Daisy Coon, and Charles McKendry; (standing) Principal Dodge, Mark Field, Blanche Sheppard, Berdie S. Zingg, and Jessie Chase.

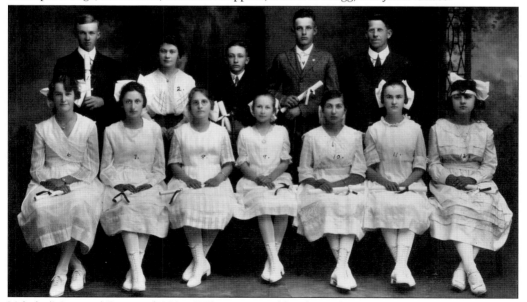

Valeda (Mattison) Burgess (1890–1977) was a granddaughter of pioneer John Stead Mattison and the eldest child of Ralph J. and Amey D. (Thurber) Mattison of Soquel. A Soquel School graduate, Valeda returned to teach. She stands, second from left, with the 1919 graduating class. Valeda is credited with gathering the Soquel Pioneer and Historical Association collection. Many names and descriptions written on the backs of photographs are in her handwriting.

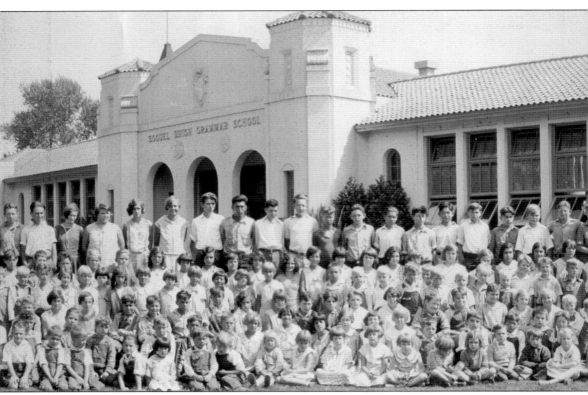

The Mission Revival–style Soquel Elementary School was designed in 1921 by public school architecture specialist William Henry Weeks (1864–1936). He believed good architecture influenced the aesthetic sense of children and enhanced their learning abilities. Soquel School received an annex in 1934 with two classrooms and a cafeteria planned by another famed architect, William W. Wurster (1895–1973). That same year, the old, two-story 1890 grammar school was razed as a CWA (Civil Work Administration) project. Today the Soquel School District's Main Street Elementary School, Soquel Elementary School, and Santa Cruz Gardens Elementary School feed into New Brighton Middle School in Capitola. (Courtesy of John Nicol.)

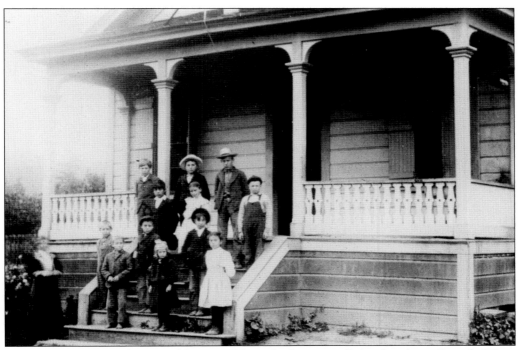

In 1866, Benjamin Cahoon and his son, Edwin, built a sawmill 4 miles above Soquel. When stumps were cleared, the family constructed a spacious house on their 960-acre Fern Gulch ranch. Edwin leased Camp Capitola in the early 1880s. He then created his own resort. Mountain School, above, was built nearby and served for several decades as both school and social recreation hall. Destroyed in 1908, it was rebuilt soon after on Soquel San Jose Road. It was given a stone and stucco exterior, below, in 1922. No longer a school, it is today the Subud House. The present 1972 Mountain School remains in a one-school district. Other rural schools that once existed near Soquel were Hazel Brook at Rodeo Gulch, closed in 1914; Glen Haven in the hills above Main Street; and the 1898 Capitola School, also shut down in 1914.

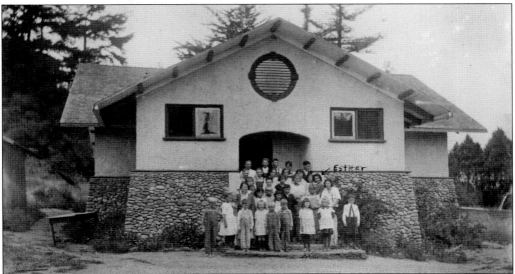

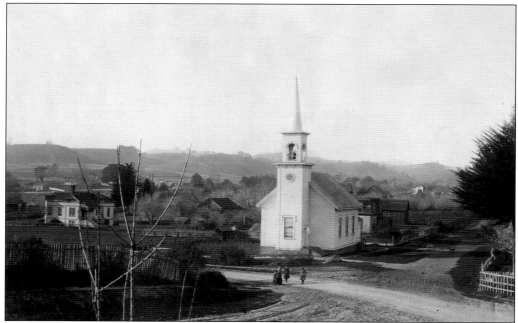

Pioneers Joshua and Narcissa Parrish discovered their home was in an isolated spot on the east side of Soquel Creek. Getting to church in Santa Cruz was particularly difficult, so Narcissa organized a prayer group for the neighborhood. The Congregational church was built in 1868 on land donated by the Parrishes at Soquel Drive and Center Street. Ship builder Samuel Alonzo Hall—soon to become founder of Camp Capitola—designed the church and oversaw its construction. The c. 1888 photograph below is a classic early view of the Soquel Valley, encompassing the Parrish orchards, the steepled white church, and the downtown village.

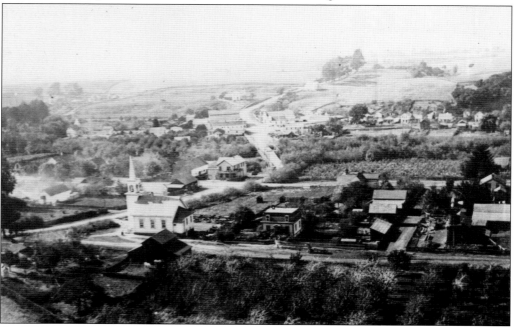

Located at Main and Bridge Streets, the Methodist Episcopal church served Soquel worshippers from 1888 until 1915. The congregation then merged with Boulder Creek. The Soquel building was dismantled and portions used for a Methodist church in Santa Cruz. The site was sold in 1920 to the Christian Science Association.

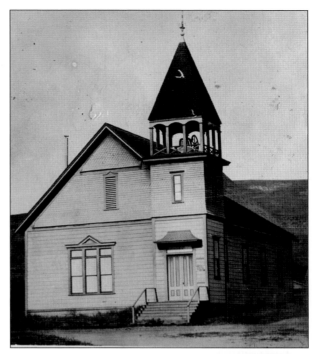

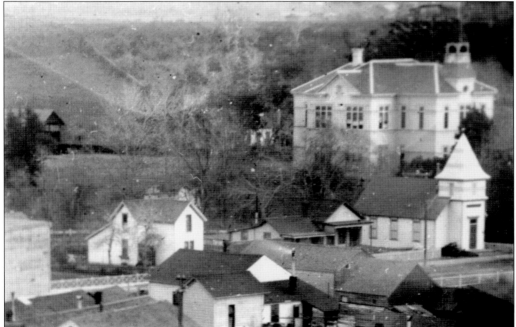

Seventh-day Adventists met in homes beginning in 1885. The church was organized in 1891, and four years later, William Kropf donated a site on Porter Street. The church is shown at lower right. It was demolished after the damaging floods of 1930–1931, and a replacement served until 1948. A new building at Porter Street and Soquel Wharf Road was dedicated on January 1, 1949. Enlarged in 1957, it was remodeled in 1989.

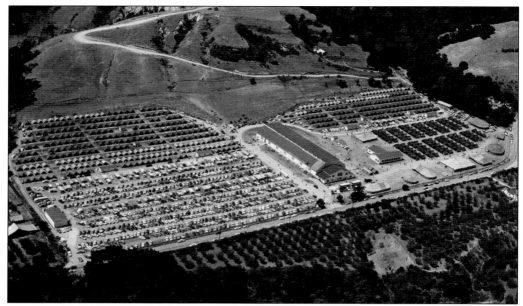

In 1947, the Central California Conference of Seventh-day Adventists bought a war surplus building for a conference center on an 87-acre parcel on Soquel San Jose Road. The structure was dismantled and reassembled for an auditorium with a 4,500-person seating capacity, ready for the annual summer camp meeting of August 1948. Today camps are generally held in mid-July, with attendees from throughout Central California and up to 15,000 participants on weekends.

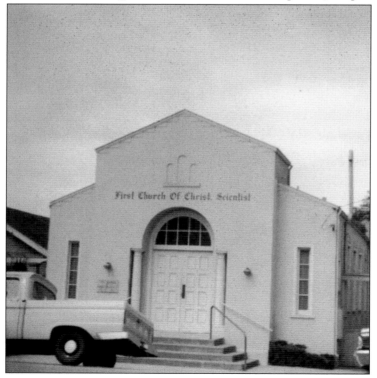

A Christian Science study group began meeting in the Benjamin Parrish home in 1916. After the First Church of Christ Scientist was organized, construction began in 1926 on a church building on Porter Street. Before completion, however, the church burned and was then rebuilt. It was damaged later in two floods. A 3-acre site on Center Street was acquired in 1966, and a new church was built in 1972. (Courtesy of First Church of Christ Scientist.)

Land for the Soquel Cemetery on Soquel San Jose Road was donated in the 1850s by pioneer John Daubenbiss, and numerous founding families are buried there. Today the older, sometimes elaborately carved headstones rest alongside contemporary ones. It is a non-endowment care park that shares space with a crematory and the Eternal Home Cemetery owned by Temple Beth El. The grave of Drucilla Shadden Hames (1833–1862), wife of Soquel founder John Hames, is marked by an older headstone. The photograph below includes the headstone of Soquel pioneer Joshua Parrish. (Right, photograph by Bill Roberson.)

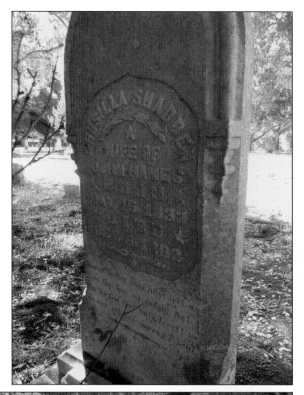

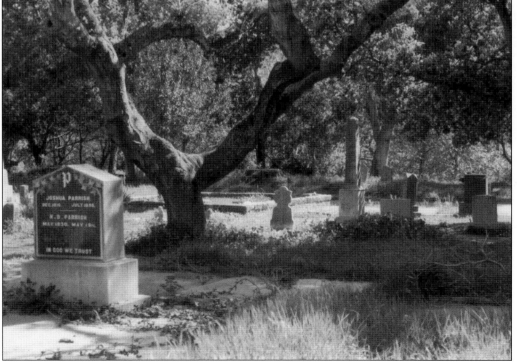

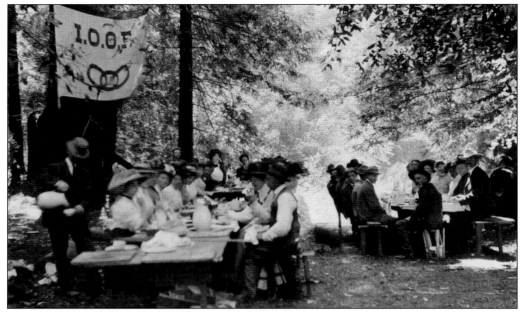

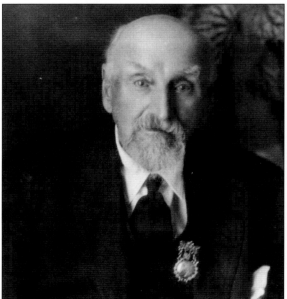

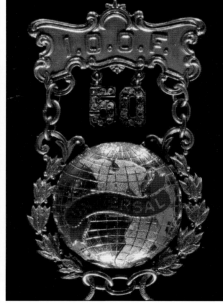

Founded in 1867, the Soquel Lodge of the International Order of Odd Fellows (No. 137) and Rebecca Lodge were actively involved in the dedication of the Porter Memorial Library, the upkeep for Soquel Cemetery, and numerous social and recreational events, such as the picnic above at Pringle Grove. The lodge built an impressive downtown hall in 1876. It was remodeled in 1913 by Soquel architect Lee Esty but lost during a fire in 1926. Esty designed the current IOOF building in 1928. Richard Nutter (1839–1924), left, was the longest continuous lodge member at the time of his death. In 1918, he received the 50-year, diamond-jeweled Odd Fellows medal inscribed, "Presented to Richard Nutter, PG, by Soquel Lodge No. 137, initiated December 14, 1868." (Photographs below courtesy Richard Nutter.)

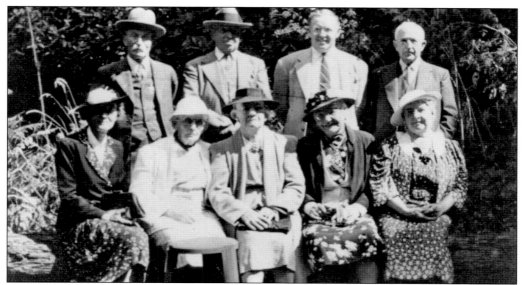

Soquel Pioneer Club's executive committee poses during the July 1941 picnic. From left to right are (seated) Bertha Marquess, Della West, Julia (Daubenbiss) Collins, Jessie (Bennett) Heath, and Nora (Oliver) Angell, the 1939 founder and first president; (standing) Silas Ryder, Uriah Thompson, Fred McPherson Jr., and Horatio Angell. On the club's fifth anniversary, Lloyd and Anne Pringle, owners of the historic Pringle Grove, announced their donation of the property.

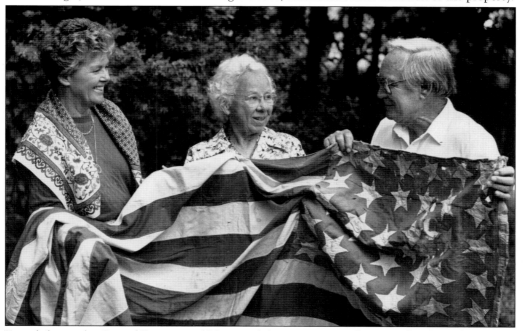

From left to right, Soquel Pioneer and Historical Association members Marilyn (Pringle) Nutter, Ceedola (Parrish) Duff, and Jay Webb prepare to display the 30-star flag to celebrate the organization's 50th anniversary. Lillie (Grover) Bibbins made a gift of the flag, which was sewn by her mother in 1886. Bibbins presented it to the Soquel Pioneer Club at the 13th annual picnic, and it remains today in the collection.

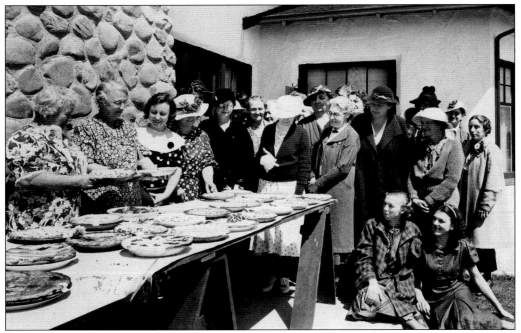

As long as cherries were abundant, pie festivals were a Soquel tradition. Monterey Bay Heights Golf and Country Club on Fairway Drive was the setting for an early-1930s event held with hotel chefs acting as taste testers. After the judging, the audience bought pies to go with a potluck lunch. Prizes were awarded in "matron" and "maid" pie baking categories. For many years, a cherry festival queen was also chosen.

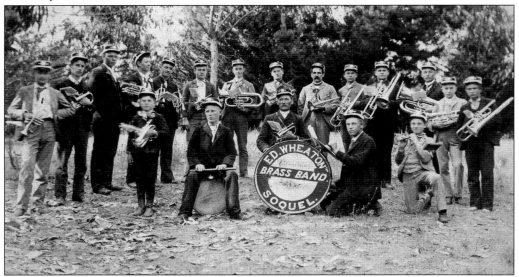

Soquel music teacher Edwin Wheaton, behind the drum, gathered with his band for a portrait at New Brighton on September 17, 1892. From left to right are (first row) unidentified, Tom Curran, Clarence Peck, and Johnnie Miller; (second row) John Broadwood, Thurman Angell, Charlie Peck, Lee Esty, Oscar Chase, Willie Bohemes, Johnnie Cunningham, Everett Gilmore, Addi Wyman, Fred Stoddard, Luther Fleckner, Schuyler Peck, Horace Mason, and Lucien Henderson.

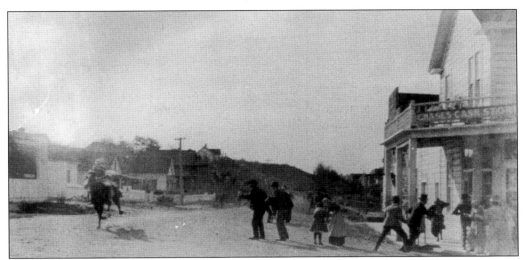

Soquel and the New England–style architecture of the town's Congregational church attracted early filmmakers. This still shot is from the 1926 version of *The Johnstown Flood*, a movie featuring, as uncredited extras, young Carol Lombard and Clark Gable. Soquel scenes were also filmed for *Rebecca of Sunnybrook Farm* (1932), *Way Down East* (1935), and *The Forest Rangers* (1942).

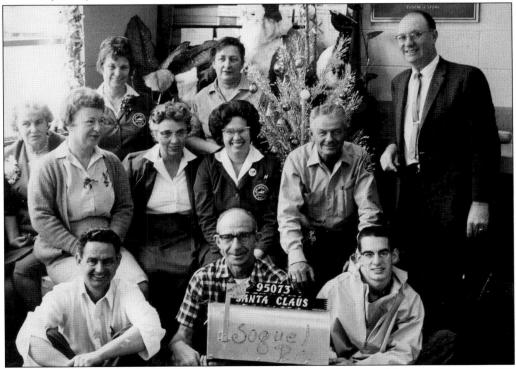

Ned Porter became Soquel's first postmaster once mail delivery began at his general store in 1857. The office location shifted over the years but stayed on Soquel Drive, where it remains today. Marion Russell Hobbs (1916–1979), postmaster for 20 years, is standing at right in this 1960s picture. Hobbs was president when the Soquel Pioneer Club transitioned to become the Soquel Pioneer and Historical Association, expanding its membership to include non-pioneers.

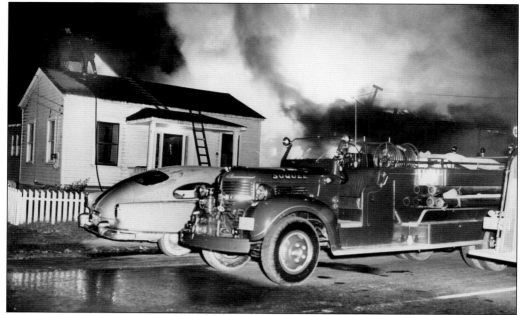

Soquel's fire department was organized in the early 1940s. In 1946, fire commissioners selected Ray Negro as chief and his brother, Ernie Negro, as assistant chief. Santa Cruz County provided an old civil defense siren and—for $1—the first truck, a 1932 Ford. The present station was built in 1957. The photograph was taken that year at a fruit-processing plant fire on Soquel San Jose Road. (Courtesy of the Central Fire District.)

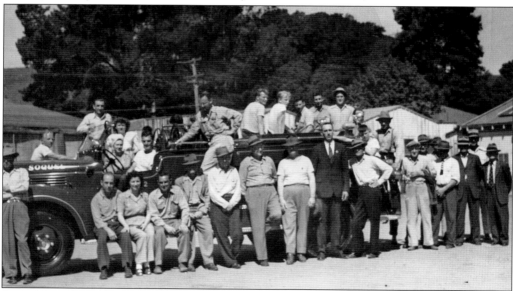

Soquel raised $7,700 in 1948 for a Dodge pumper. From left to right are (first row) Art Morgan, Ray Negro, Gemma Negro, Nip Dallas, Phil Girrard, Arno Fidel, Henry Stricker, Frank Oettl, and four unidentified; (second row) Al Gafvert, Mel Rushton, Barbara Negro, Lillian Rushton, Ernie Rebuffo, Jack Oney, Bud Fidel, Dean Fidel, Frank Beccaria, Ernie Negro, Ray Rebuffo, Warren Wessell, unidentified, and Ace Oney. (Courtesy of Steve Negro.)

Seven

TAKING IT EASY
FUN, SUN, AND FOG

Nothing has put Soquel in brighter focus than pictures of people having fun. Even giddy children could be frozen into expressions of dour seriousness by the shutter lag on early cameras. A glimmer of merriment was still apt to shine through when the occasion was happy; subjects conveyed a lighthearted cheer, a glint of humor, or a level of drowsiness—depending upon age of the subject, the hour of the day, and libations downed during the party.

Soquel's social events, particularly in the summertime, were often chilled by coastal fog. Settlers as early as 1856 referred to it as "friendly shelter" from California's hot interior. Cool mists and the mild climate attracted families seeking to protect their children from sicknesses they believed were linked to extreme temperatures.

A few vacationers came directly to Soquel, but most headed for the coast at Capitola or the other, lesser-known spots nearby, Camp San Jose (New Brighton) and Camp Fairview. Locals also took to the beach for fun. They met with companions and sampled resort pleasures—boating, sea bathing, roller skating, dancing, or listening to concerts. At day's end, they rolled back home in time to milk the cow and start supper.

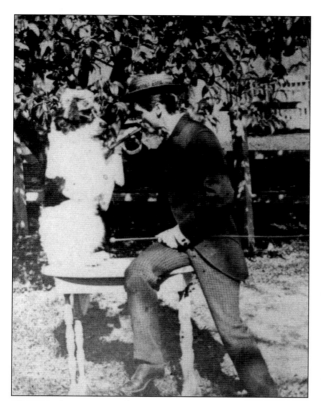

In the 1880s, William Kropf not only provided entertainment with the curios he collected and stored in his barbershop, but he often had a canine companion trained to perform tricks. He is shown here with one named Clipper.

An outdoor meal was arranged in the 1890s with the same care as an indoor one. The women shown are relaxing in the yard of a home on the O'Neill Ranch, located on the hill above Soquel Creek and the village. Louise Getzschmann, a member of the Alex Getzschmann family who owned the Park House Hotel, was married to John J. O'Neill, and members of their extended families lived on the ranch. (Courtesy of John Getzschmann.)

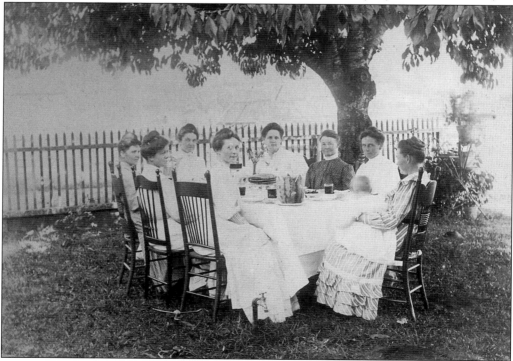

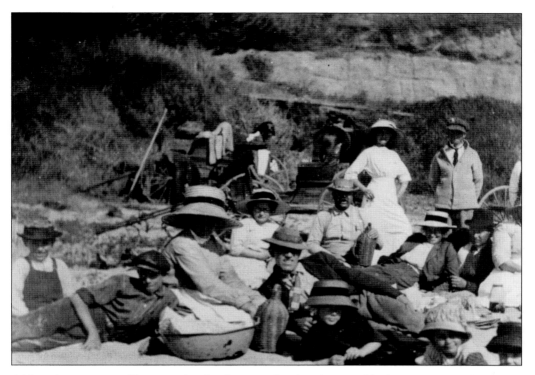

Although it was owned by Capitola's developer Frederick Hihn—and had no amenities whatever—China Beach was sometimes favored by locals. A wagon was packed with picnic gear and driven onto the sand for the *c.* 1910 family holiday shown above. Soquel's Camp Fire Girls, below, enjoyed the cove in the early 1920s. Among those identified are Marion Nutter, far left; Clara Nutter, center, with Helen Anderson; and Margaret Maddock, center right. (Above, courtesy of the Hazel Bardt family; below, courtesy of Richard Nutter.)

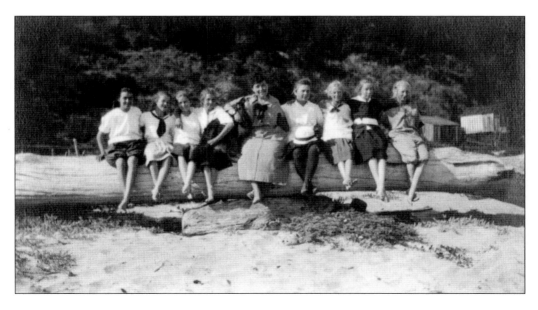

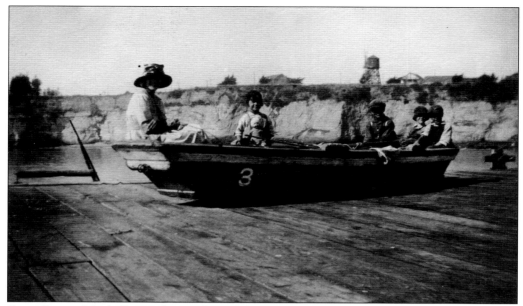

Capt. George Mitchell rented out a fleet of skiffs at Capitola from 1895 until he retired in 1945. The captain also took fishing parties out on his launches, the *Capitola* and the *Betsy*. Clara Nutter, left, relaxes on one of the Mitchell skiffs with her children—from left to right, Helen, Marion, and Burton—onboard with Helen Anderson, a friend, about 1919. (Courtesy of Richard Nutter.)

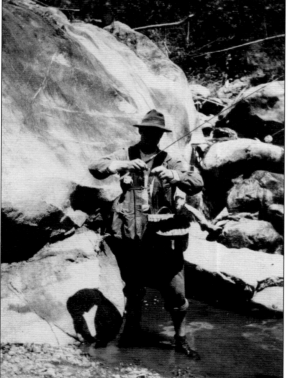

Soquel Creek was known for abundant trout. Sport fishing was enjoyed by both adults and children. In some years, opening day was a school holiday. Fishing limits were imposed when the stream became overfished; in later years, the maximum was 25 per person, per day. Olley Nutter is ready to cast his line on the west branch of Soquel Creek in the 1920s. (Courtesy of Richard Nutter.)

Edith Pawla, owner of Pawla's Violet Gardens on Wharf Road, lived on property that she and her daughter, Emily, called Happy Hill. Both were self-reliant and proud of improvements they made to their home, including plumbing installation and electric lights. One day, the two heard steelhead splashing upstream below their terraced garden. Edith pulled on a swimsuit and proceeded to "wrestle" their supper to shore. (Courtesy of Shirley Coleman.)

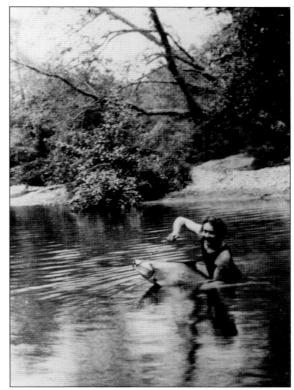

Edith and Emily Pawla's "violet wonderland" was planted with 4,000 trees. Edith even grew Royal Hawaiian palms from seeds picked up off a sidewalk in Los Angeles. This c. 1920 photograph shows Emily with one of the English sheepdogs they raised. Edith is on their horse. Their automobile was rare in the era of black Ford Model Ts—it was custom-ordered in violet. (Courtesy of Shirley Coleman.)

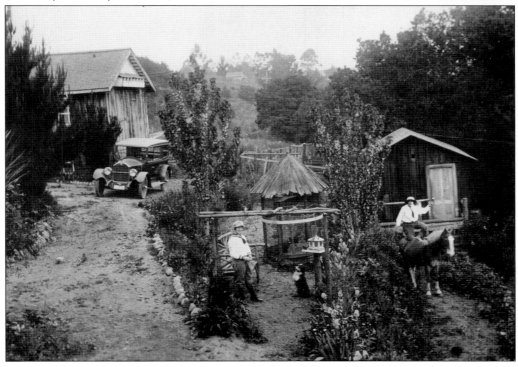

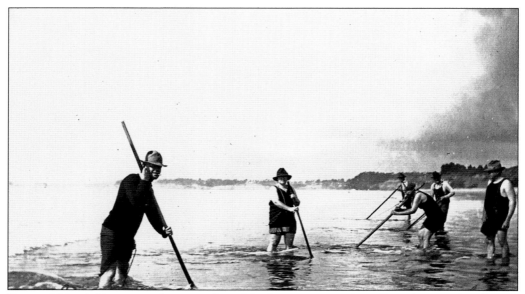

Don and Maude Emery, ranchers near Laurel in the mountains above Soquel, spent their leisure time hunting and fishing. In this 1921 photograph, the family and friends are digging for clams in the surf near Aptos. (Courtesy of Horton Kooser.)

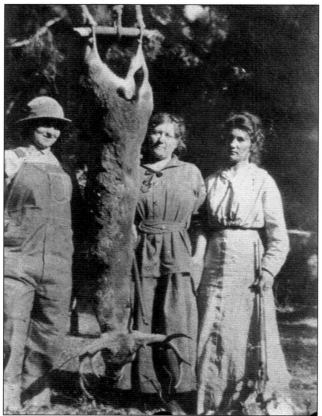

Rifles in hand, Maude Emery and two female companions stand with a deer they killed during a hunt about 1915. Deer were numerous in the vicinity until the mid-1900s, when expanding population reduced their habitat. Today deer still roam the wooded canyons in and around Soquel, having adapted to encroachment by humans. (Courtesy of Horton Kooser.)

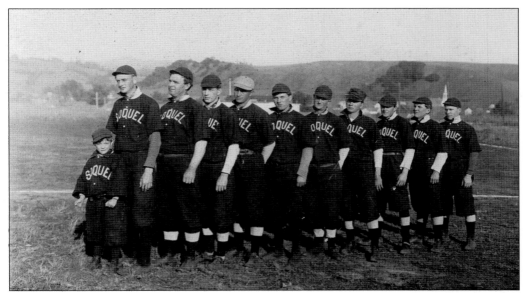

This 1911 picture of the Soquel Giants is the best known local team image. Future Baseball Hall of Fame inductee Harry Hooper wears the white hat. Team members are, from left to right, mascot Jack Malloch, Harvey Nugent, Clarence Angell, Milton Nugent, Harry Hooper, Harvey Bradley, Tom Hickey, Jack Bostwick, Eugene Daken, Branch Wallace, and Paul Johnston. Several players became civic leaders.

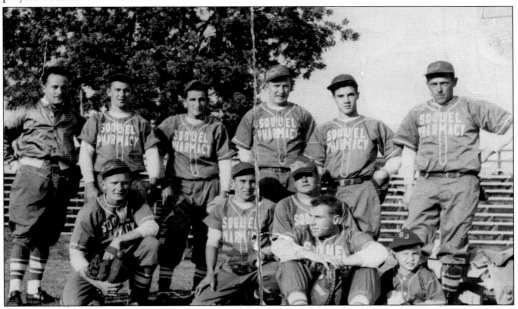

Eventually, businesses backed home teams and provided uniforms. The 1950 Soquel Pharmacy team above was a mix of college-age men and slightly older players who competed in Santa Cruz City League games held at the Santa Cruz High School football field. Shown from left to right are (first row) Arno Fidel, Ernest Negro, Raymond Martin, Richard Finta, and Thomas Finta; (second row) Delmar Miller, Richard Nutter, William Casalegno, Fredrick Fidel, Darrell Millsap, and Donald Gravelle. (Courtesy of Richard Nutter.)

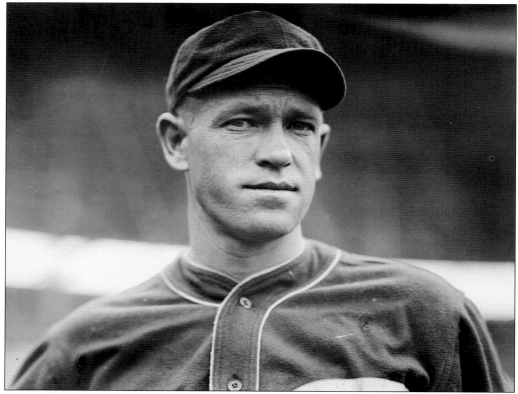

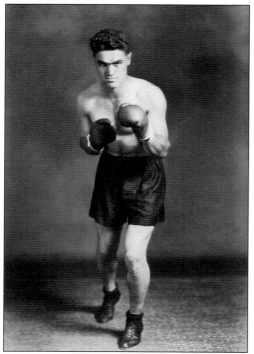

"The Black Prince of Baseball" played in Soquel. One of baseball's great talents, and also one of its great villains, Hal Chase was raised above Soquel, where his father operated a sawmill at Cahoon's Gulch. He attended Soquel Grammar School and became a star for the New York Yankees. Babe Ruth characterized him as the greatest first baseman of his era. But he was also an incorrigible drinker and gambler whose antics got him banned from the game. (Caption and photograph courtesy of author and historian Geoffrey Dunn.)

During the 1920s and 1930s, professional boxing provided an important source of Saturday night entertainment in Santa Cruz County. The darling of Soquel pugilists was light heavyweight Jesse DeMotta, who boxed under the name of "Jess DeMotte" from 1926 to 1931, compiling a 14-10 record with eight knockouts. His brother Glenn was also a popular boxer (6-1-1). (Courtesy of the DeMott family; caption by author and historian Geoffrey Dunn.)

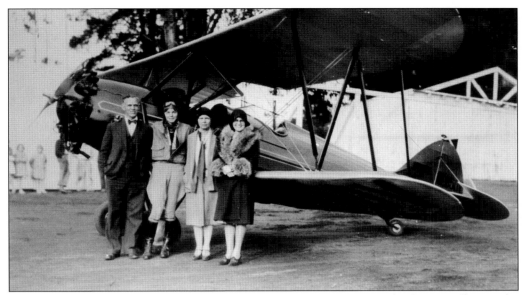

In her mid-20s, Edith (Bond) Fikes (1909–1991) became an aviator and a frequent flyer at the Santa Cruz–Capitola Airport. Bond (second from left) poses at the airfield with her parents and sister. After Edith had married Walter E. Fikes and was an owner of the historic Soquel Inn, her flying experience paid off; the hotel was a favorite with pilots and their spouses. (Courtesy of the Capitola Historical Museum.)

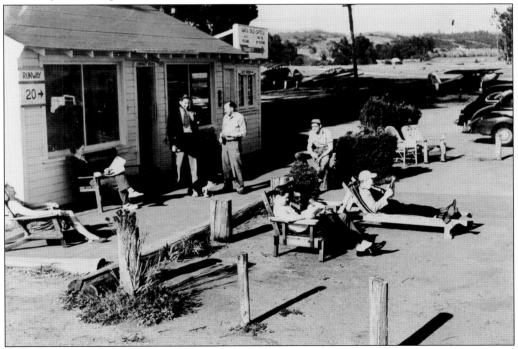

Soquel resident Russell Rice, standing center right, learned to fly when a glider club started using the field along the coast. Rice took over as airport manager in 1945. He and his wife, Esther, operated the municipal airport until it closed in 1954. (Courtesy of Covello and Covello Photography.)

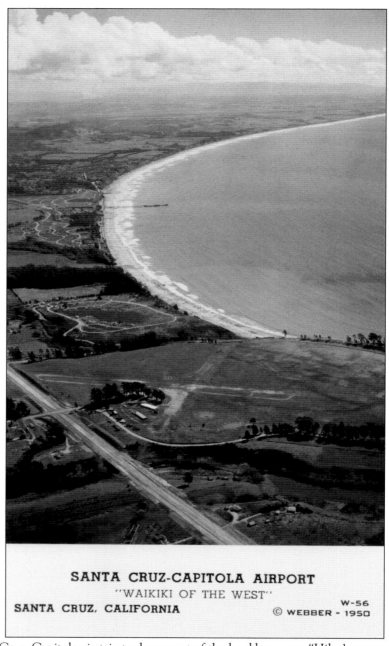

SANTA CRUZ-CAPITOLA AIRPORT

"WAIKIKI OF THE WEST"

SANTA CRUZ, CALIFORNIA

W-56
© WEBBER - 1950

The Santa Cruz–Capitola airstrip took up most of the land known as "Hihn's eastern field." The site became a popular spot for glider pilots in the late 1920s. In 1926, the site was designated as the Santa Cruz Municipal Airdrome. The National Guard Artillery encampment known as Camp McQuaide was established nearby at the same time. In 1934, the Santa Cruz–Capitola Airport was constructed as a WPA project. The 1950 Ed Webber photograph, promoting the coastline as the "Waikiki of the West," was taken after Highway 1 was completed. In the center, just beyond the airport, is New Brighton Beach State Park. The farmlands in the foreground and to the left of the airfield were a part of Soquel. (Courtesy of Covello and Covello Photography.)

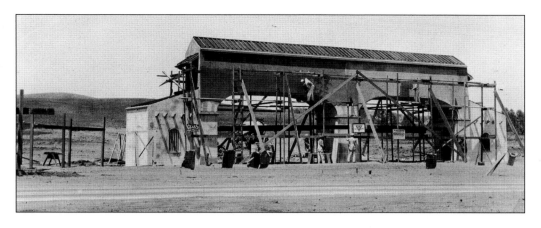

When San Francisco speculator H. Allen Rispin (1872–1947) bought Capitola in 1919 from the heirs of Frederick Hihn, he also acquired 200 acres in Soquel. Rispin's Capitola Company predicted quick profits through a series of auctions that marketed vacation lots "by the sea." By 1927, however, the venture was failing. Rispin's last-ditch scheme was a golf course on his Soquel property. In the above photograph, workmen finish the Monterey Bay Golf and Country Club's arched entrance on Soquel Drive. Robert Hays Smith, an investment partner, took over in 1931 but went bankrupt five years later. Airplanes occasionally landed near the golf clubhouse, which was converted later into a private residence. Today it is a long-term care facility. (Courtesy of the Capitola Historical Museum.)

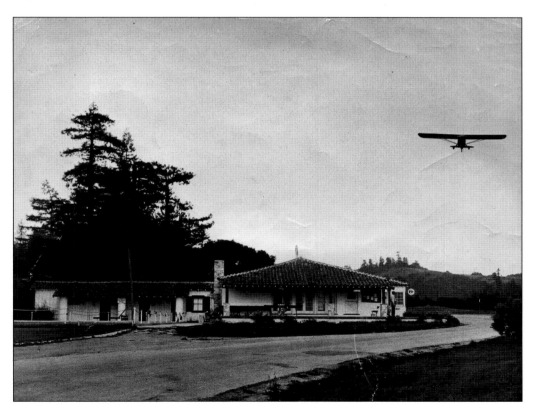

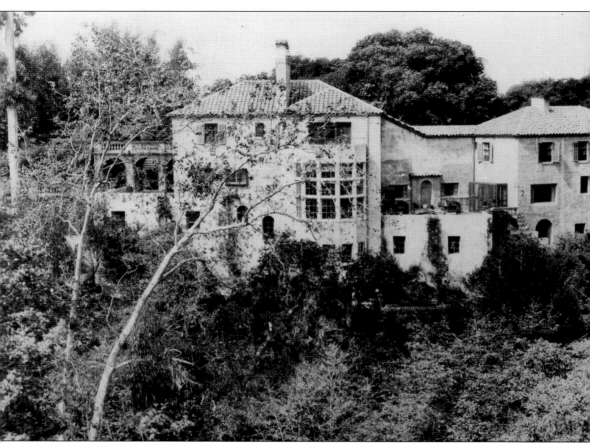

When Rispin bought Capitola, he spent $4,000 for a dam on Bates Creek that supplied Capitola and Soquel with water. Frustration with the capitalist's subsequent management was a primary reason leaders from both villages decided in 1928 to explore the creation of a joint municipality called Sotola. Although merely an idea on paper, it drew attention to financial failings of the Capitola Company. Monterey Bay Golf and Country Club was Rispin's last big project. He announced at one point a plan to convert his Wharf Road mansion to serve as the golf course clubhouse. Instead, he sold his home and the golf course to Burlingame millionaire Robert Hays Smith. In 1941, the mansion became the Order of Poor Clares Convent. The nuns had left by 1957, and the house sat empty until purchased by the City of Capitola in 1986. Still vacant, it burned in 2009. (Courtesy of the Capitola Historical Museum.)

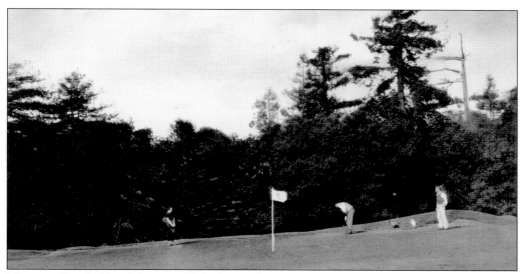

Monterey Bay Golf and Country Club, shown above, struggled throughout the Great Depression and World War II, closing in the early 1950s. In April 1951, Thomas Prescott created the Eaglewood Golf Club nearby. With nine holes, Eaglewood was considered a challenging course. The clubhouse at the end of Fairway Drive in the Monterey Bay Heights subdivision is today a private home. (Courtesy of the Capitola Historical Museum.)

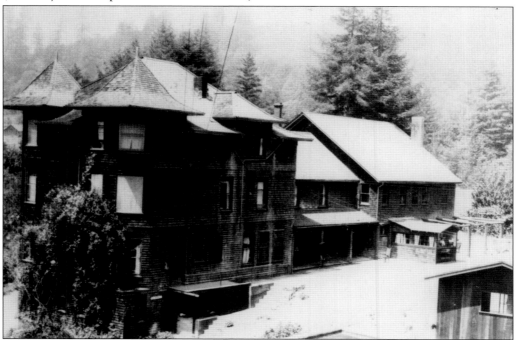

Set in the foothills near Bates Creek, Stafford's Inn initially boarded loggers and sawmill laborers. Walter Stafford refurbished it as a retirement retreat in the early 1900s, adding cottages, a bar, and dining and recreation rooms. In 1918, George Prescott bought the resort and ran the inn with the help of his wife, Mary Jane Hammond Prescott, and children Thomas, George Jr., Dorothy, Sarah, Edith, and Elsie.

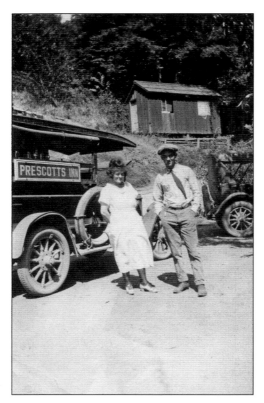

The Prescott name was given to both the resort and the road leading to it. Advantageously situated in the foothills—2 miles from the beach and normally above the fog line—Prescott's Inn gave vacationers the best of both worlds. Rides to Capitola were offered in its "limo," shown with siblings Tom and Elsie Prescott. The resort offered swimming, riding, hiking, sports, and evening campfires. (Courtesy of Sylvia Prescott Forsyth.)

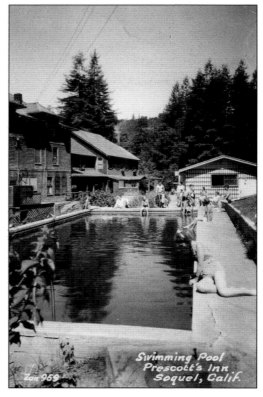

In 1939, the resort became Denton's Mountain Inn, owned and operated by Linder and Zelda Denton (known as "Pop" and "Mom"). In 1962, the historic four-story structure burned. Two years later, Bill and Elsie Beltram acquired the remains of the resort and built the conference facilities known as Greenwood Lodge. Since the early 1980s, it has been a retreat called Land of Medicine Buddha. (Courtesy of the Capitola Historical Museum.)

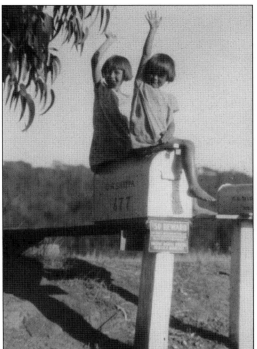
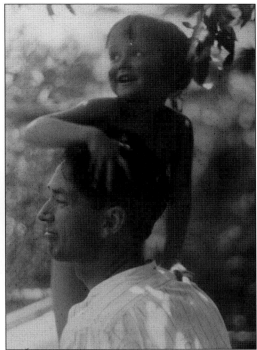

R. Irving Lovett holds his daughter Joanne in *Under the Peach Tree*, photographed in 1929 by famed photographer Dorothea Lange on the Sheppa/Lovett property along Soquel Creek. Irving's wife, Louise Sheppa Lovett, was an artist friend of Lange. The *c.* 1930 photograph of the Lovett girls, Mary Louise (left) and Joanne, on top of the family mailbox was taken by Lange. (Photographs by Dorothea Lange; courtesy of Joanne Lovett Lathrop.)

Max and Marion Caldwell founded Kennolyn Camp in 1946, named for their children Kenneth and Carolyn. Since many of their first attendees were nieces and nephews, the couple became "Uncle Max and Aunt Marion" to thousands of campers, counselors, parents, and staff. Kennolyn Camp became known worldwide as a summer experience offering activities described in their brochure as "In the Redwoods near the Sea." (Courtesy of the Caldwell family.)

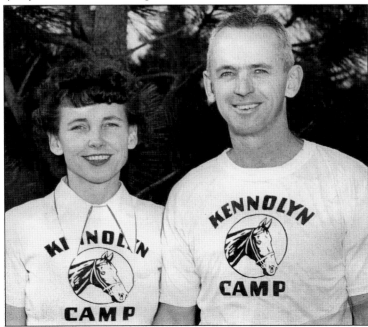

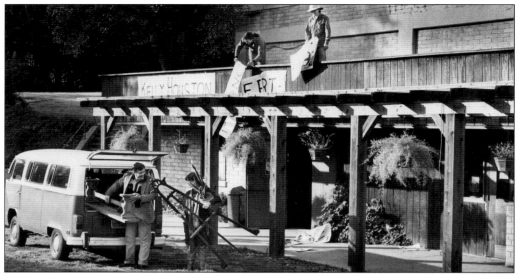

After Joseph Jacobs opened the Capitola Theater in 1948, he was asked to start another in Soquel. Osocales Theater had 500 seats and a babies' crying room. The cinema lasted three decades before its curtain closed. The building reopened briefly as an adult movie house. It next offered live performances as West Abbey Theater, above. Since the mid-1980s, the structure has been Lighthouse Christian Church. (Courtesy of the Capitola Historical Museum.)

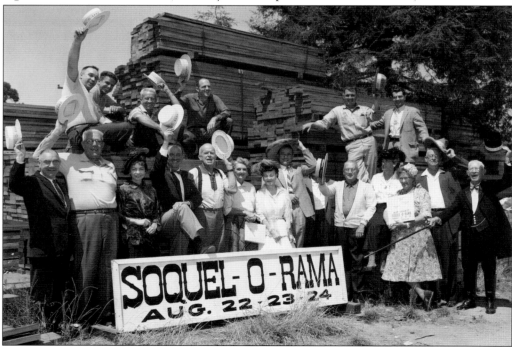

Created by the Soquel Optimists and other local business clubs, the Soquel-O-Rama was a folksy celebration organized in the 1950s to attract visitors during the warmer temperatures of early autumn. The 1959 planning committee is shown at a kick-off meeting. The lively festival continued irregularly through the 1980s. (Courtesy of Covello and Covello Photography.)

Eight

DISASTERS
FLOODS, FIRES, AND QUAKES

Inside the Soquel Porter Memorial Library, two walls are marked with lines. One traces the high water of the 1955 flood within the building, while the other measures the height of the 1982 flood. And these floods are only the most recent.

When raging water tore through the landscape in 1862, shopkeepers realized they had a problem. The town sat in a basin. To improve the situation, they lugged in dirt, shifted the roadway, and built structures higher off the ground. But downtown was still in lowland. Adding to the danger were bridges and flumes that hung low, snagging logs and brush sweeping downstream. Despite efforts to hook and pull away the debris, the creek clogged and the banks overflowed.

The community came together in these times of crisis. Greeting bleary-eyed neighbors over coffee before yet another soggy clean-up day was customary in the 1930s and 1940s. Floods happened so often that before long people confused one year's mishap with another.

Earthquakes have shaken buildings, rattled nerves, and left scars throughout the county. The magnitude 7.8 epicenter of the San Francisco earthquake of 1906 was 90 miles away, but it had tragic consequences for Soquel. In 1989, the 6.9 magnitude Loma Prieta earthquake was centered but a few miles away, with emotional impact lingering long after the mess was cleared.

Fires were also frequent and wearisome. News of an uncontrolled blaze in the hills brought teams and wagons from all directions to help save the timber, grain, and livestock. In town, ringing church bells could mean either a call to weekly services or a calamity.

Soquel has recovered from many of its disasters with the help of friends. When Soquel was hit by the 1982 flood, Capitolans gave donations to help clean up. A year later, when a high tide pummeled the Capitola Esplanade, the favor was returned.

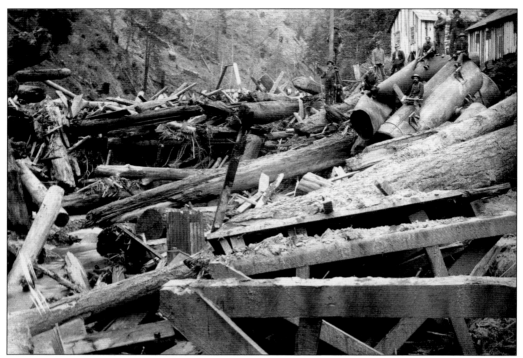

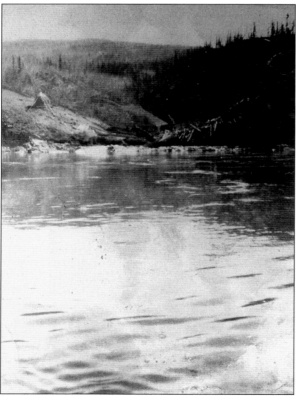

Loma Prieta Lumber Company's sawmill on Hinckley Creek, near Olive Springs, was destroyed in a January 1906 storm. This photograph shows the damage. Reconstruction was underway when, on the morning of April 18, an earthquake and a mudslide slammed the mill's cabins while men slept inside. The next day, the bodies of August Long, Alexander Morrison, Frank Jones, and Henry Estrade were recovered. Victims Fred Peaslee, J. O. Dunham, A. Buckley, and J. W. Walker were found later. Some bodies were too deep to be recovered. Charlie Jun, the camp's cook, was never located and is believed to have escaped. Earthquake Lake, left, was created when a depression in Hinckley Basin filled with rainfall in the weeks after the earthquake. (Above, courtesy of Big Creek Lumber Company; left, courtesy of Jerry Stoodley.)

LOMA PRIETA LUMBER CO.

190 _____ *To* _____ *Dr.*

	See attachment,			
4	days time, self & assistant	12.00	48.00	
	first dive		20.00	
	second & third descents	10.00	20.00	
	railroad fare, San Francisco to			
	Capitola and return		11.20	
	expressage		15.60	
			114.80	

G. O. ABRAHAMSEN

...SUBMARINE DIVING...
In All Its Branches

MOORINGS RECOVERED

Union Iron Works
WITH L. FOARD
Phone Main 670   No. 9 Steuart Street
* * *
156 Fulton St RESIDENCE
526 HARRISON STREET
Phone Black 276   SAN FRANCISCO, CAL.
Phone Montgomery 1483.

1906

MA PRIETA LUMBER COMPANY,

_____ Dollars,

G O Abrahamsen

Donkey engine under 30 ft of water back of slide on it 50 Diver pulls line on it had another donkey 190 team haul it out

Loma Prieta Lumber Company's donkey engine was in 30 feet of water at the back of the mass after the 1906 earthquake. A handwritten note on the bill above indicates that $114.80 was paid to G. O. Abrahamsen Submarine Diving. Two divers were sent into the lake to attach lines to salvage the submerged engine. The photograph below shows the donkey engine after it was raised from the lake. (Above, courtesy of Jerry Stoodley.)

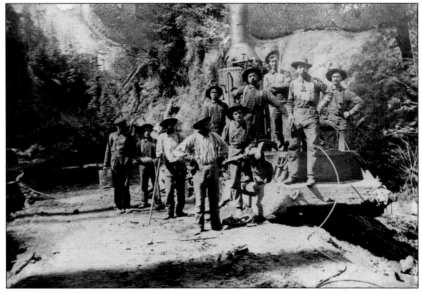

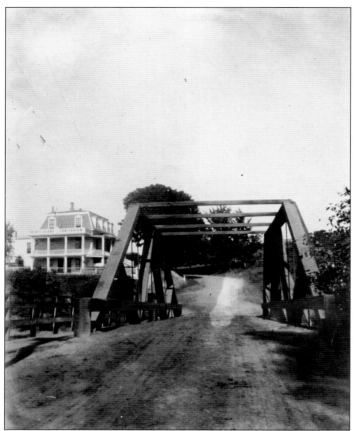

Soquel Grammar School pupils were at their desks on November 6, 1912, when they heard a loud cracking noise. Looking out the windows, they witnessed—and many never forgot—the Walnut Street Bridge, left, crashing into Soquel Creek. The accident happened while driver Ike Ripley, injured and seated on the wreckage (below, far right), was driving a team of five horses and a load of apples to the Nutter Apple Dryer. The span was never rebuilt. In the late 1980s, however, local citizens were inspired to recreate the Walnut Street Bridge for pedestrians only. Today it leads from the schoolyard to the Lion's Club Park on South Main Street. The collapsed Bridge Street Bridge has since been similarly rebuilt for the benefit of foot traffic.

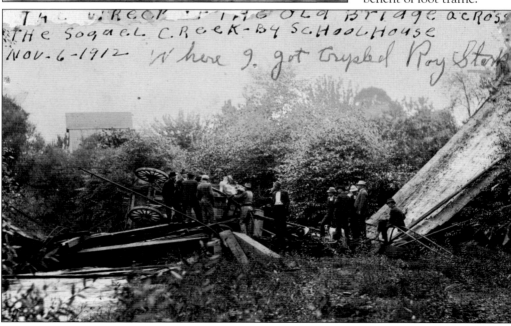

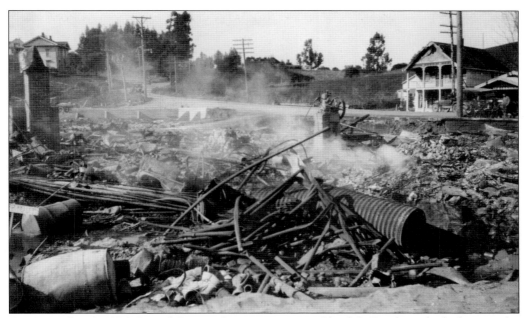

On December 6, 1926, Soquel Service Station proprietor Lloyd C. Boydston looked across the street and saw flames shooting from an empty building behind the IOOF Hall. He set off an alarm and called Santa Cruz firefighters for help, but the flames spread fast, consuming the entire block. County supervisor Addi Wyman later blamed a deficient water system supplied by the Capitola Company of H. Allen Rispin. (Courtesy of the Capitola Historical Museum.)

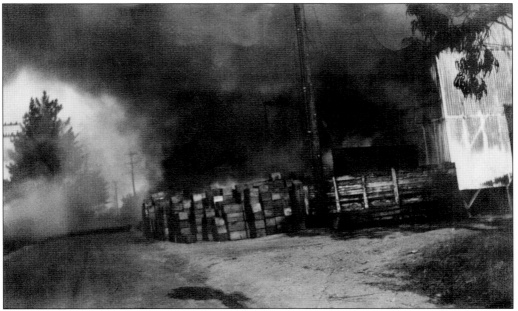

A harvest of apples rested next to the burning Nutter Apple Dryer warehouse in 1931. The dryer and vinegar works, established by Olley Nutter, was a longtime Soquel industry. The Nutter family continued to live on their nearby ranch along Hill Street in present-day Capitola. (Courtesy of Richard Nutter.)

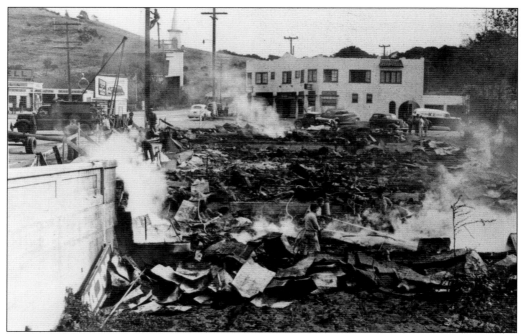

A fire in November 1940 destroyed nine commercial buildings belonging to Lewis Dingwall on Soquel Drive at South Main Street. A tenant upstairs in the Kasseroller building across the street had spotted and reported the blaze, but the water pressure was not strong enough to quell the flames. (Courtesy of the Capitola Historical Museum.)

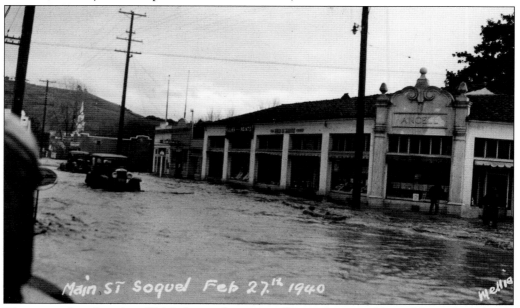

The new and modern Angell's Market, at the corner of Porter Street and Soquel Drive, had already been hit by floodwater several times before February 27, 1940, the day the photograph was taken. Businesses were once again inundated as the creek jumped its banks and rushed down Soquel Drive, turning south to rejoin itself along Porter Street.

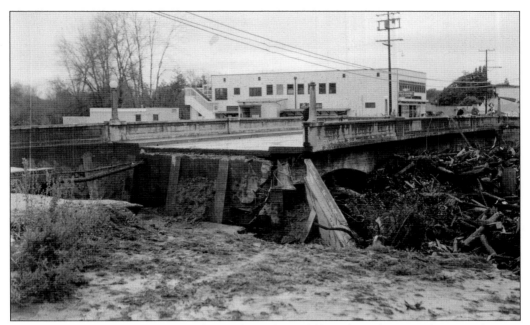

Just before Christmas 1955, more than a foot of rain fell in three days. At the Soquel Drive Bridge, remains of a four-room house and five cabins joined the rubble that wedged against the bridge abutments, causing the bridge to collapse. Overall damage to Soquel and Capitola property exceeded $1 million. (Courtesy of Covello and Covello Photography.)

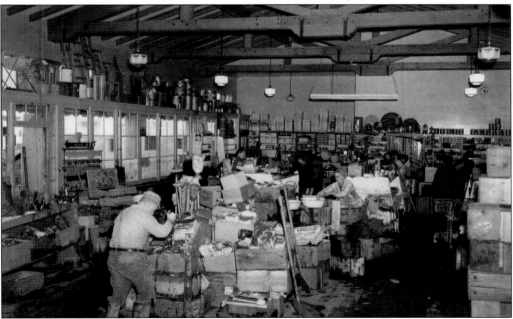

The former Angell's Market had become Willbanks Brothers Red-and-White Store by the time of the 1955 flood. As was the custom, employees and customers worked together to sop up the mess. The high water came back in 1982, when the building was the Soquel Branch of County Bank, and it suffered the same consequences. (Courtesy of the Willbanks family.)

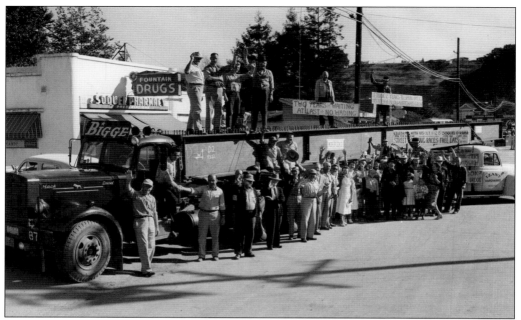

After the bridge at Soquel Drive was destroyed in 1955, motorists had to travel many miles out of their way to get across town. Weary of the detours necessary to cross Soquel Creek, citizens were ecstatic in 1957 when work finally began on the improved span. (Courtesy of Covello and Covello Photography.)

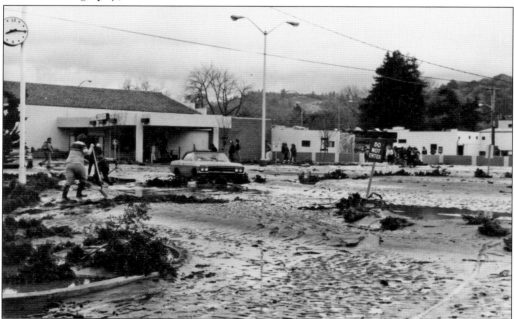

As soon as the water receded on January 5, 1982, volunteers began reclaiming Soquel from the mud. The bridge at Soquel Drive was damaged by a 100-yard-long logjam. It was replaced in a $3.5-million renovation project completed in 2002. Known today as the Lawrence Bargetto Bridge, the new span sits 2 feet higher over Soquel Creek. (Courtesy of Carolyn Swift.)

Nine

CHANGING TIMES
SHAPING THE FUTURE

California faced numerous challenges in the postwar years, among them an expanding highway system, a booming population, development pressures, incoming cultural influences, and shifts in education. The most difficult adjustment for Soquel was a veritable boundary change. In 1949, the asphalt barrier of the new Highway 1 and the incorporation of the City of Capitola placed physical and legal dividers between Soquel and the beach resort that had once shared its history.

In the 1950s, the Soquel community struggled with familiar tests of endurance as well as new, unforeseen threats to its way of life. The 1955 flood was another of the perennial natural disasters to leave an indelible mark on the landscape. Damage was so great that the town initially endorsed an Army Corps of Engineers flood-control project proposal offered in 1961.

Two years later, however, residents realized that a central part of the flood-control project was the building of an earth-filled dam that would create a 1,000-acre lake above town. Protesters formed the Association for Preservation of Soquel Valley in 1963. It became one of the first local citizen action groups to galvanize public opinion on preservation and environmental issues. As a result, the dam was never built. Soquel Creek Water District, initially established as part of the project, continues to serve the water needs of more than 50,000 customers in Soquel and neighboring communities.

Disputes over housing development proposals became more numerous in the 1960s. By the time discussion began in 1972 on revisions to the 1961 Santa Cruz County General Plan, residents were aware that they needed to voice their concerns. Citizen groups, such as the Soquel Highlands Improvement Association, the Soquel Valley Association, and Concerned Citizens for Soquel, were leading advocates of growth control. Slowly Soquel was transforming itself to cope successfully with the complex hurdles of a new era while maintaining its historic character.

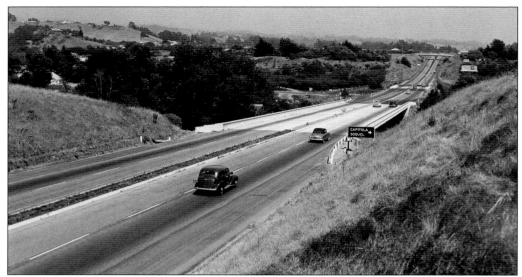

In 1941, construction started on a modern highway to connect Santa Cruz and Watsonville. The work began in South County and reached a point near Aptos when Pearl Harbor and World War II shut the project down in December. Delayed until 1947, the job resumed with crews laboring to complete within two years the stretch to Morrissey Boulevard on the outskirts of Santa Cruz. The final link, connecting to Highway 17, was finished in 1958. The historic Averon house, below at the top left, previously in Soquel, is now within the Capitola city limits. Both pictures date from the early 1950s. (Both, courtesy of Covello and Covello Photography.)

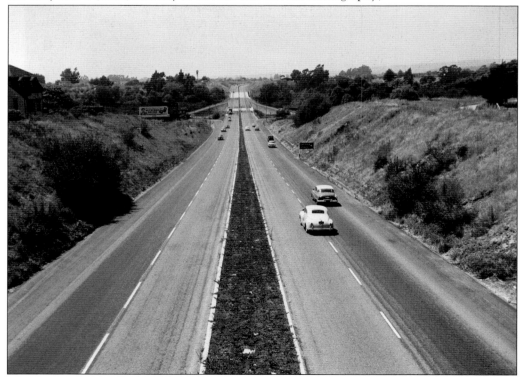

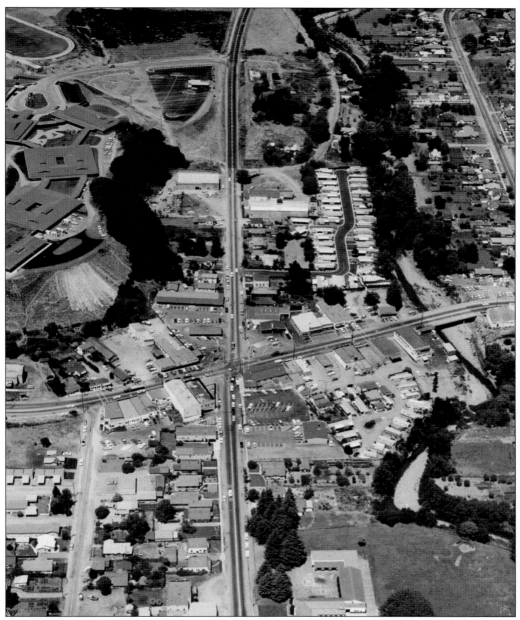

An early-1960s aerial view captures the beginnings of urban encroachment within the Soquel Village core. Although housing infill impacted the older neighborhoods, the downtown commercial district retained its character. The "X" formed by Soquel Drive and Porter Street marks the historic crossroads. Soquel High School, top left, was built in response to school overcrowding due to increasing development. The photograph also illustrates the spread of new construction to former agricultural lands. Soquel Creek skirts the play yard of Soquel Elementary School at lower right. (Courtesy of Covello and Covello Photography.)

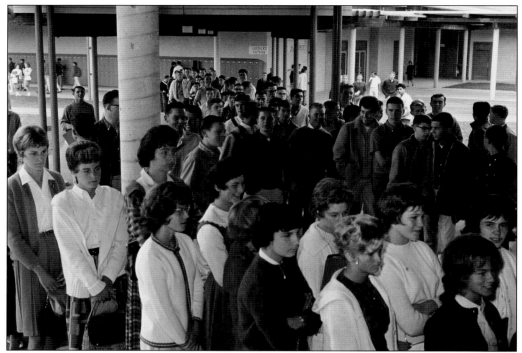

Santa Cruz and Watsonville high school enrollments expanded with each incoming freshman class. In 1959, Santa Cruz Unified School District voters passed a school bond measure providing for the construction of a "mid-county high school." The 50-acre site was a hillside parcel on the O'Neill Ranch. Students were welcomed to Soquel High School for the first day of classes in the fall of 1962. (Both, courtesy of Covello and Covello Photography.)

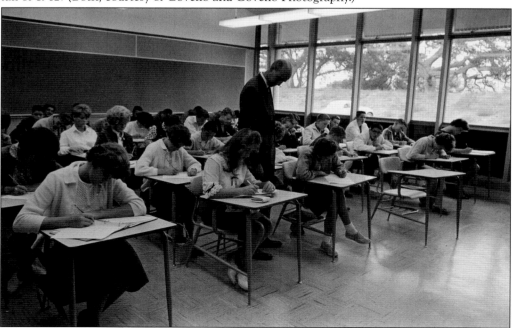

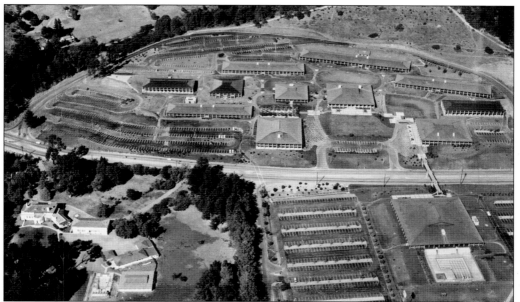

Santa Cruz and Watsonville overcame long-standing rivalries to approve plans in 1958 for a two-year college in mid-county. A site search was underway by the time Cabrillo Junior College opened in temporary quarters at Watsonville High School in 1959. A 100-acre section of the Sesnon property was purchased in 1961. The postal address was changed to Aptos, although the campus remains within traditional Soquel boundaries. The Sesnon Mansion (above, far left), across the road from the main campus, was acquired by the college in 1974 for use as its Community Education Center. (Above, courtesy of Covello and Covello Photography; below, photograph by Sam Vestal, *Watsonville Register–Pajaronian* photographer, courtesy of Carolyn Swift.)

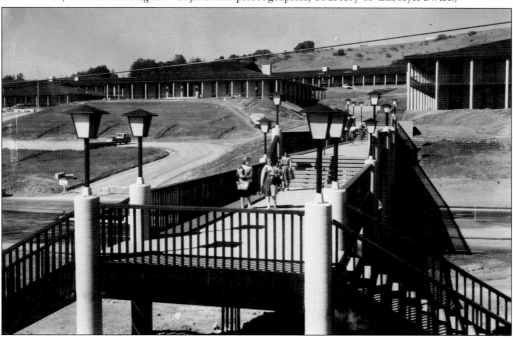

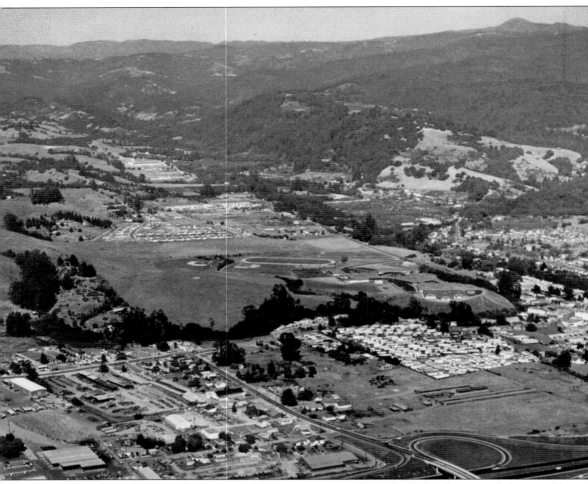

Debates for and against development became intense in the early 1970s. A proposal that would have tripled Soquel's population led to the formation of the Save Soquel Committee in 1973. Its members won significant victories by turning back proposed developments on the O'Neill Ranch property. The committee is best remembered for its campaign begun in 1979 against a 537-unit housing proposal. In the photograph, the oval Soquel High School track (center) marks the general O'Neill Ranch project site. Conflict eased when Santa Cruz County agreed in 1988 to purchase a portion of the land with redevelopment funds. More than $2 million were spent toward land costs. Community forums in the early 1990s had a significant impact on the scope of the project. (Courtesy of Covello and Covello Photography.)

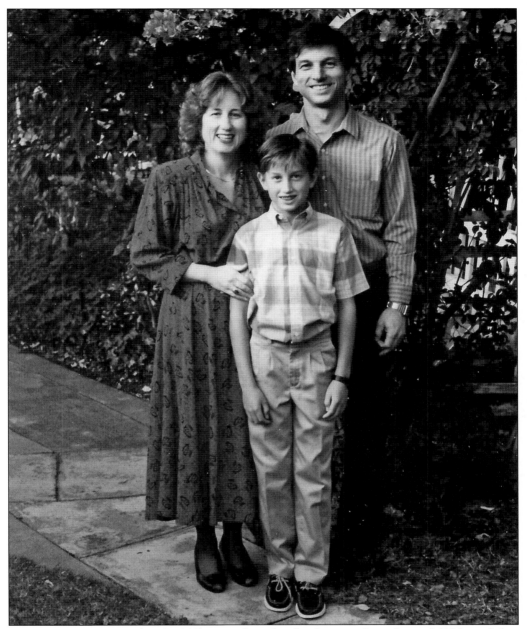

Anna Jean Cummings (1946–1990) poses for a family photograph in the mid-1980s with her husband, Bill, and son, Brian. She was a Save Soquel founder and executive committee member and also the first executive director of the Santa Cruz County Land Trust. Cummings was honored for her longtime activism when the park was named in her honor in 1990, the year she died. Park construction began once a recreation master plan was approved in 1998. Four enormous blue balls were installed along the hillside for an art project completed a few years later, giving the playground area its nickname "Blue Ball Park." Its official title, however, is the Anna Jean Cummings Park, respecting her achievements in the 25-year effort to preserve the O'Neill property. (Courtesy of Bill Cummings.)

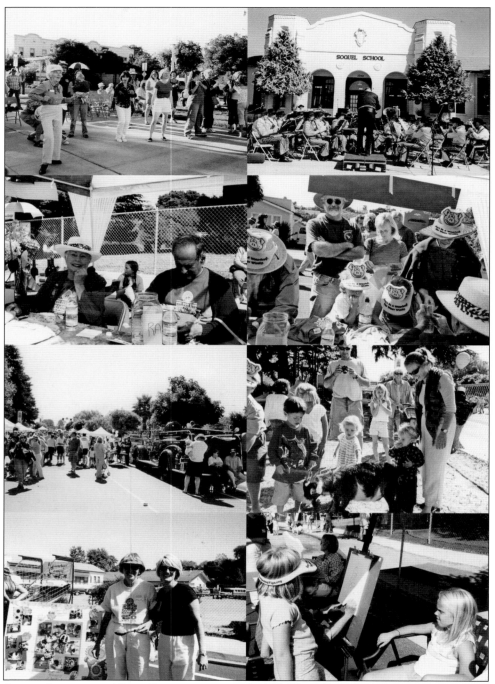

A festive observance of Soquel's sesquicentennial was held in the summer of 2002. Porter Street, above, was closed for festivities that included an antique car display, musical performances, vendors, and a barbecue. Tours were given of historic sites. Photographs and keepsakes were placed in a time capsule honoring the town's 150th birthday, and it was imbedded in the new Lawrence Bargetto Bridge. (Courtesy of Jill B. Hall.)

Ten

REMEMBER WHEN
THEN AND NOW

Soquel has never been "off the beaten path." Traffic stops can be interminable. And in this town, a sharp appreciation for the pace of modern life can be achieved simply by stepping off the sidewalk curb.

Trying to pinpoint the same location shown in an old photograph by pacing around in the middle of Soquel Drive is to discover that "looking backward" is a phrase to be taken literally. In any one of Soquel's intersections, dancing between cars with a camera requires vigilance, good eyesight, agility, and a superfast shutter speed.

Results are worth it. Even where exact matches cannot be made, the pairings of "then" and "now" are photographic witnesses to time's impact on the landscape. Orchards vanish. Buildings appear and disappear. Roadways become straightened, widened, and paved. Some places look better than before, others are not so good, and a few have barely changed paint color.

Transformations reveal themselves. The rhythm of growth around Soquel Village remained slow and steady for generations before World War II. The tempo picked up speed the instant the war ended. Arriving young families required housing, amplified the need for more schools, and swelled the intersections with hundreds of cars.

Although cursed during commute hours, the road through town is nevertheless its oldest landmark. Tracing the contours between the Soquel Congregational Church on the east end and the Daubenbiss house to the west, Soquel Drive runs a line from present to past, visually joining the two structures that give the village its historic identity.

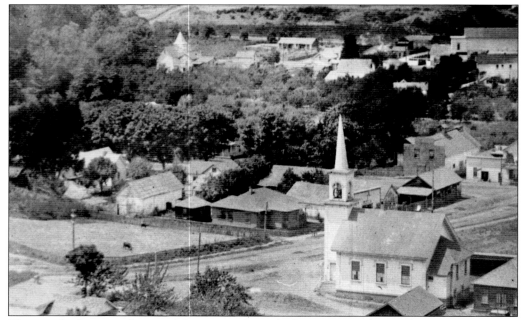

The standard postcard view of downtown Soquel, above, is aimed toward Santa Cruz, taken after traffic had increased enough to warrant widening Soquel Drive. The road narrows at the bridge over Soquel Creek. Orchards touch the roadway on both sides. Expansion of subdivisions and the growth of trees have made it more difficult to capture a modern comparative view. The achievement today requires permission to stand on rooftops in the Parrish Hill neighborhood.

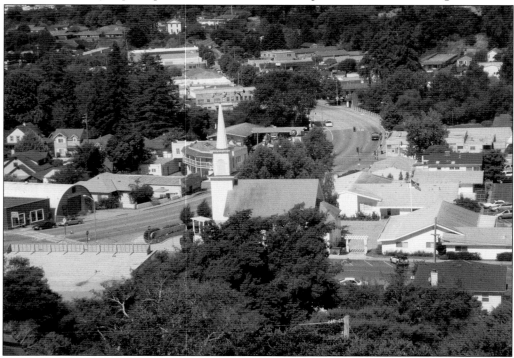

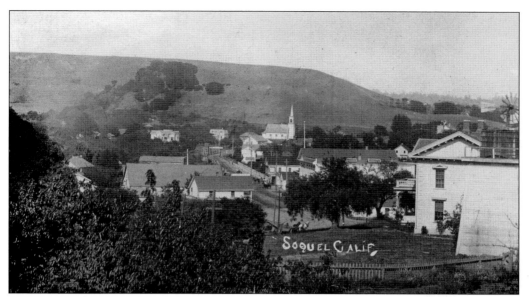

No trees stand on Parrish Hill directly behind the Congregational church in this postcard view, taken about 1910 looking east from the Daubenbiss house at far right. John Daubenbiss built the house himself in 1867 with the help of George Eldridge and Henry Bischell using redwood lumber. The Soquel Drive roadbed was later cut lower to make an easier grade. Over the years, the house has been a home, a halfway house, and a bookstore. Today it is once again a private residence. The bottom image, taken from Robertson Street at Soquel Drive, shows the white steeple of the church. The Daubenbiss house is hidden behind the trees to the right.

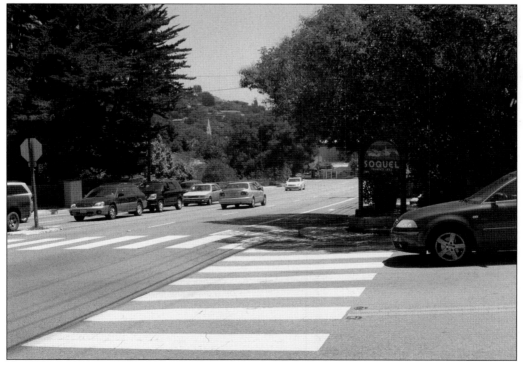

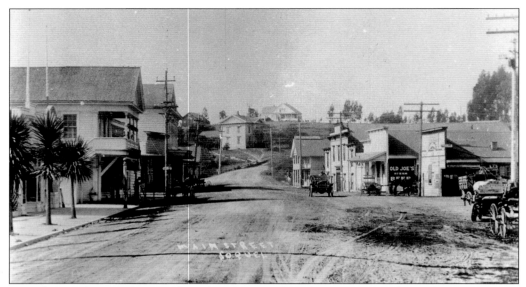

Soquel was a farming district when this photograph of the Porter Street/Soquel Drive junction was taken about 1912. Ruts were cut into the roads by wagons loaded with produce. The lone automobile approaching the Porter Street and Soquel Drive intersection could putt along at about 8 miles an hour with plenty of room and the freedom to go wherever the driver wished, on either side of the road. Automobiles were fairly common in Santa Cruz County by then, but most were owned by drivers wealthy enough to afford both the car and the cost of keeping it on the road. Today, in contrast, the intersection is all about cars.

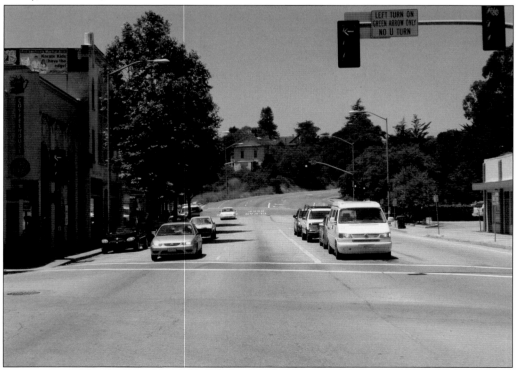

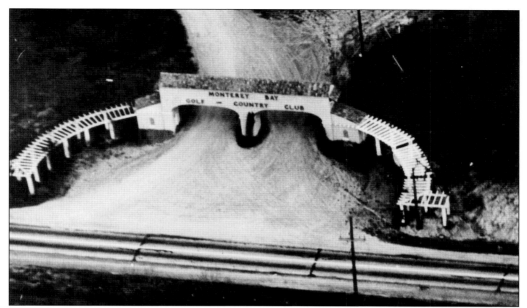

Soquel Drive was a 15-foot-wide rural country road in the stretch between Soquel and Aptos during the 1920s. In contrast, the sweeping entrance to H. Allen Rispin's Monterey Bay Golf and Country Club appeared absurdly broad with its imposing stucco archway. Improved roads over the mountains boosted tourism in Soquel and Capitola and made the golf course a feasible attraction for vacation homeowners. (Courtesy of the Capitola Historical Museum.)

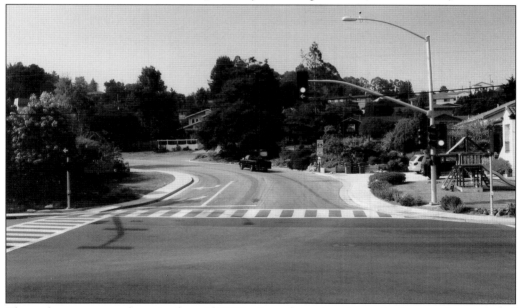

The arches were torn down in the mid-1960s. A modern view shows the intersection as one of two access roadways into the Monterey Bay Heights subdivision. Residents live on streets with names linked to the history of Monterey Bay Golf and Country Club and the Eaglewood Golf Course. Among them are Stance Drive, Tee Street, Ball Drive, Golf Drive, Bogey Court, Par Street, Hazard Drive, Putter Drive, Jigger Drive, and Fairway Drive.

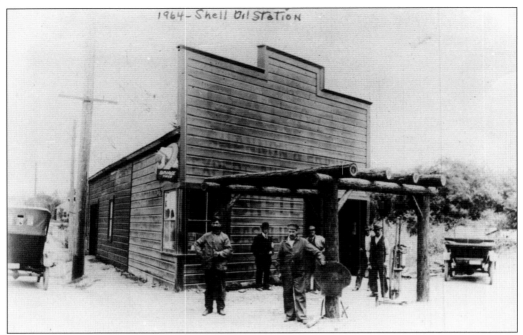

Located at the northeast corner of Porter Street and Soquel Drive, the building above was Shannon and Pringle's X-Ray Garage and gas station. Originally the site of Sam's Senate Saloon, the structure was a longtime landmark in spite of its plain architectural style. Standing in the photograph are, from left to right, Jack Shannon, Bill Halliday, owner Lloyd Pringle, Lincoln Dawson, Al Smith, and Royal Egbert.

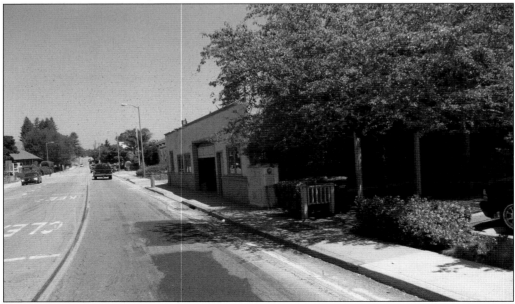

A custom automobile restoration business near the corner echoes today the simple style of the gas station and the legacy of blacksmith, wagon, and car repair garages that once existed at this crossroads. The building on the far right now houses the Soquel Center offices.

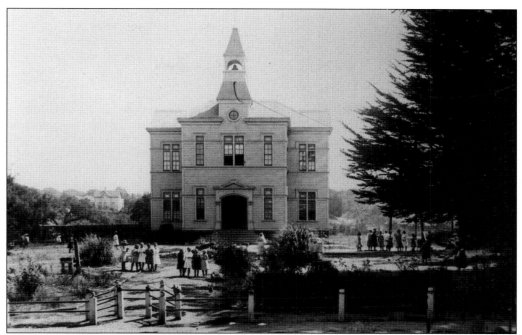

Soquel's redwood, two-story school was built in 1889 with an open belfry and spire. On top was a 25-foot flagpole topped by a 14-inch copper ball that had been a time capsule, made by Alfred Bowman, containing names of students, teachers, and trustees. An "old-timer's night" was planned when the ball was removed 45 years later, but it was discovered that a marksman had used it for rifle practice and the documents had crumbled. After the school was demolished in 1934, the annex shown below was added to the 1921 elementary school next door.

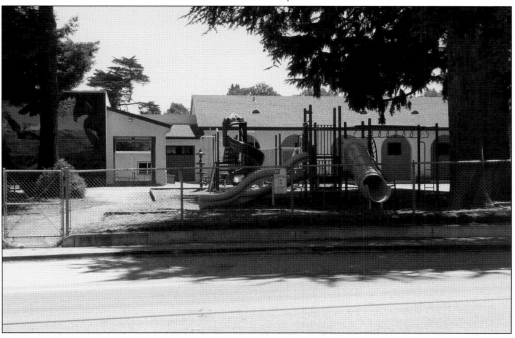

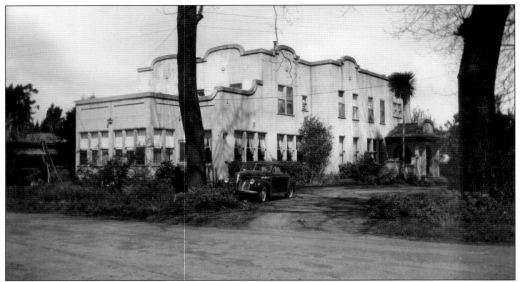

In 1865, Alexander "Alex" Getzschmann and Agnes Kusterling were married in Soquel. Shortly afterward, the couple took over the ownership of the Park House Hotel on Porter Street. A native of Vienna and trained in culinary arts, Agnes quickly built up a following among the townspeople and workers from surrounding mills. Alex planted black walnut trees along the corner at what is now Walnut Street. Entertainers who signed in as guests included minstrel show performers, musical comedy troupes, and at least one fortune teller. Over the years, Edith and Walter Fikes expanded and renovated the hotel, reopening it in 1945 as the Soquel Inn. Today the historic building is the Old Soquel Plaza complex, with a new addition that mirrors the original architecture.

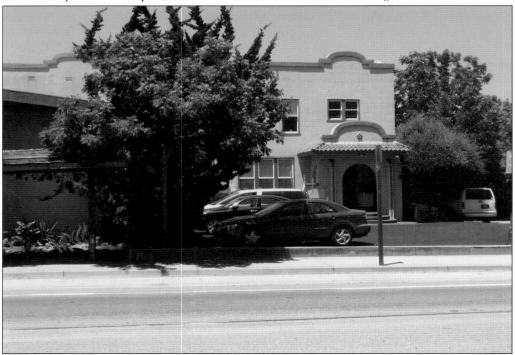

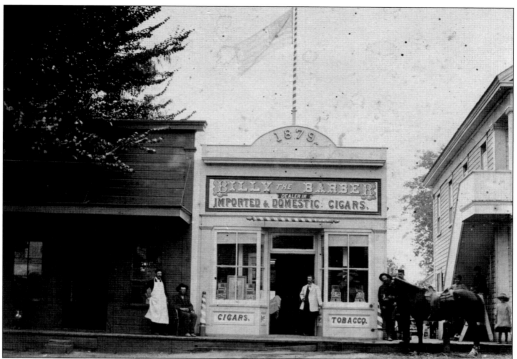

In the 1870s, William Kropf opened a barbershop in Mann's Hotel. By 1879, he had his own place as "Billy the Barber," where he also sold tobacco products and kept a display of curios that entertained his waiting customers. Billy was well liked. His shop was popular as a gathering spot for men with idle time—almost as popular as the saloon. Today a shave and a haircut can be had in practically the same spot at the Hairy Chair on Soquel Drive.

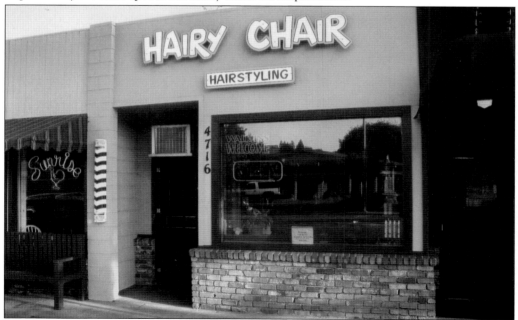

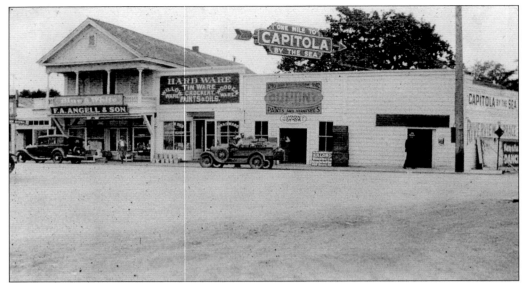

F. A. Angell and Son operated their store on the corner of Soquel Drive and Porter Street for 57 years. The 1930 photograph above includes several directional signs for Capitola, indicating the volume of tourist traffic that came through the intersection on the way to the beach. Clarence Angell replaced the market with a new structure in 1932. Ray Willbanks bought it in 1944 and, with Earl and Jack Willbanks, opened Willbanks Brothers Red-and-White Store as Soquel's first modern supermarket. Remodeled several times—and usually after a flood—the store later housed Midtown Market, County Bank of Santa Cruz, Pacific Western Bank, and Comerica. It is now Soquel Village Antiques. (Above, courtesy of Ted Maddock.)

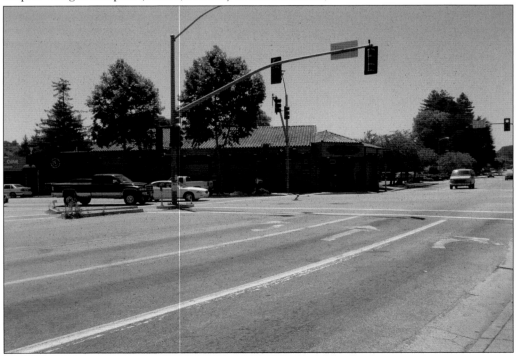

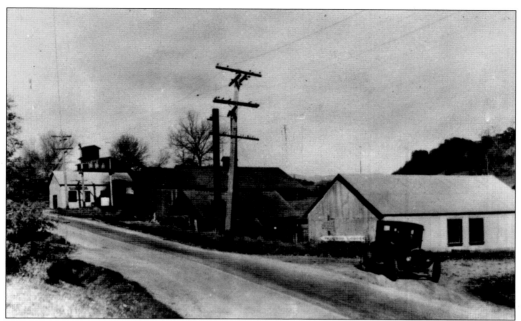

Remnants of the historic flour mill built by John Hames and John Daubenbiss were incorporated into the South Coast Paper Mill near the corner of Bridge Street and Paper Mill Road in 1879. This is the site where Lt. William Tecumseh Sherman (1820–1891), later famous as a Union general during the Civil War, spent a night in 1848. Sherman and his party had crossed the Santa Cruz Mountains and could see the firing of a salute 60 miles away at Monterey, counting the number of guns by the puffs of white smoke. The photograph above is of the mill site in the 1920s. Paper Mill Road is now a dead-end residential street that connects to Soquel San Jose Road only at the southern end, nearest Porter Street and the village.

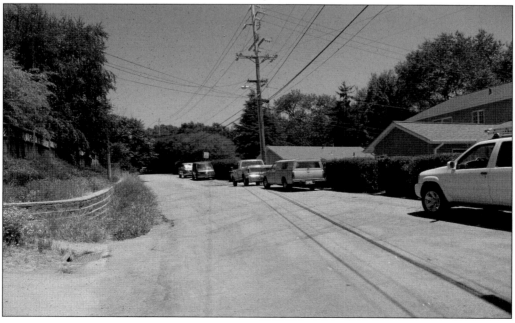

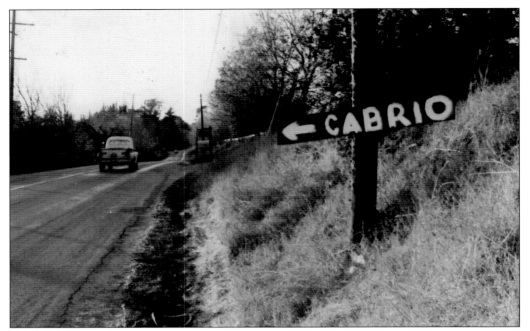

Once the Cabrillo College property was agreed upon, a sign—spelled phonetically—was hammered to a pole along Soquel Drive to guide construction crews to the site. The new campus opened with approximately 2,000 students. College expansion and renovation projects have been approved in every decade since. (Above, photograph by Sam Vestal, courtesy of Carolyn Swift.)

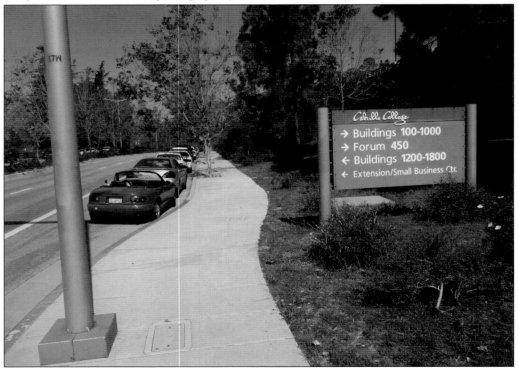

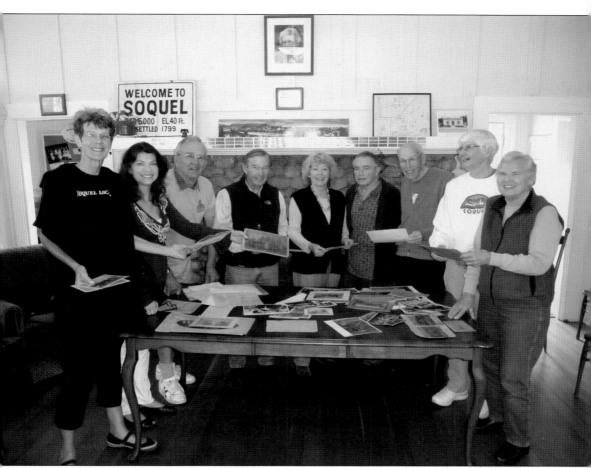

Although the flooding of Soquel Creek is a recurring theme in Soquel's past, its impact on history was dramatically illustrated when the Soquel Pioneer and Historical Association's photograph collection was saturated in 1982. Since then, members have worked to restore and preserve the images that best tell the story of old Soquel. This book culminates the effort. Shown in the Soquel Memorial Library with the mud-stained pictures are, from left to right, authors Carolyn Swift, Alice Daubenbis, Paul Parsons, Richard Nutter, Lynne McCall Caldwell, John Caldwell, Bill Roberson, Judy Parsons, and Barbara Harlamoff McCrary.

DISCOVER THOUSANDS OF LOCAL HISTORY BOOKS FEATURING MILLIONS OF VINTAGE IMAGES

Arcadia Publishing, the leading local history publisher in the United States, is committed to making history accessible and meaningful through publishing books that celebrate and preserve the heritage of America's people and places.

Find more books like this at
www.arcadiapublishing.com

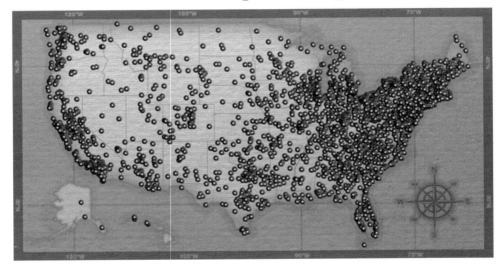

Search for your hometown history, your old stomping grounds, and even your favorite sports team.

 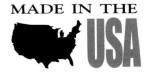